Justice, Unity,
and the Hidden Christ

# Justice, Unity, and the Hidden Christ

The Theopolitical Complex of the Social Justice Approach to Ecumenism in Vatican II

Matthew John Paul Tan

PICKWICK *Publications* · Eugene, Oregon

JUSTICE, UNITY, AND THE HIDDEN CHRIST
The Theopolitical Complex of the Social Justice Approach to Ecumenism in Vatican II

Copyright © 2014 Matthew John Paul Tan. All rights reserved. Except for brief quotations in critical publications or reviews, no part of this book may be reproduced in any manner without prior written permission from the publisher. Write: Permissions, Wipf and Stock Publishers, 199 W. 8th Ave., Suite 3, Eugene, OR 97401.

Pickwick Publications
An Imprint of Wipf and Stock Publishers
199 W. 8th Ave., Suite 3
Eugene, OR 97401

www.wipfandstock.com

ISBN 13: 978-1-62032-364-9

Cataloguing-in-Publication data:

Tan, Matthew John Paul.

Justice, unity, and the hidden Christ : the theopolitical complex of the social justice approach to ecumenism in Vatican II / Matthew John Paul Tan.

x + 108 pp. ; 23 cm. Includes bibliographical references and index(es).

ISBN 13: 978-1-62032-364-9

1. Social justice—Religious aspects—Catholic Church. 2. Vatican Council (2nd : 1962–1965 : Basilica di San Pietro in Vaticano). 3. Christianity and politics. I. Title.

BX830 1962 .T36 2014

Manufactured in the U.S.A.

Just as there are two coinages, one of God and the other of the world, each with its own image, so unbelievers bear the image of this world, and those who have faith with love bear the image of God the Father through Jesus Christ

IGNATIUS OF ANTIOCH

Contents

Acknowledgments | ix

Introduction | 1

1 *Unitatis Redintegratio* and Vatican II's Engagement with Secular Culture | 9
2 The Council, Its Presuppositions, and Postmodernity | 27
3 Liberalism, Capitalism, Church, and Ecumenism: Nexus or Battlelines? | 45
4 *Leitourgia, Diakonia,* and *Oikumene* | 62

Conclusion | 83
Bibliography | 93
Index | 101

Acknowledgments

THIS WORK IS NOT just my own. Many important people and organizations have in many ways contributed to the birthing of this book, all to whom I owe my thanks and to whom this book is dedicated.

My thanks to the Russell Berrie Foundation, whose Fellowship in Interreligious Studies provided the funding that enabled me to spend a considerable amount of time in Rome, the perfect setting for reflection on this work, considering its primary subject matter was undertaken just across the Tiber. This funding in turn afforded me contact with faculty members at the Pontifical University of St. Thomas Aquinas in Rome, otherwise known as the *Angelicum*, many of whom have also provided invaluable intellectual and administrative assistance. Special thanks are due to Rev. Dr. Carsten Barwasser, OP, who provided sage advice in the drafting process, and to Rev. Dr. Bruce Williams, OP, without whom my time at the *Angelicum* would not have been possible. Thanks also to Prof. Donna Orsuto, the staff of the Lay Centre and to Rev. Dr. Athanasius McVay, all of whom provided a home away from home in Rome. They brought together a wonderful support network, the discussions and conviviality with whom played a vital role in tilling the intellectual soil that nurtured this work. Eric Bernhard has assisted me greatly in editing the early drafts of this text.

Thanks are also due to those who foregrounded my Italian sojourn with incredible support, assistance and preparation. The first of these are my mother, Frances, and brother, Joseph. Archbishop Mark Coleridge and Monsignor Anthony Randazzo of the

Acknowledgments

Archdiocese of Brisbane have opened many doors that would have otherwise remained closed to me. Last but not least, Dr. Terry Veling of the Australian Catholic University and Prof. Tracey Rowland of the John Paul II Institute for Marriage and Family provided the intellectual discipleship that has profoundly shaped this work.

Introduction

Framing the Problem

IN *UNITATIS REDINTEGRATIO*, THE Fathers of the Second Vatican Council exhorted the faithful to engage in cooperative projects with non-Catholics as an avenue to foster visible church unity. Of particular interest in this regard was paragraph 12, in which the Council encouraged all Christians to confess their common faith in the Triune God through "cooperation in social matters" such as

> the promotion of the blessings of peace, the application of Gospel principles to social life, the advancement of the arts and sciences in a truly Christian spirit. It should use every possible means to relieve the afflictions of our times such as famine and natural disasters, illiteracy and poverty, lack of housing and the unequal distribution of wealth.[1]

That same paragraph spoke of the great benefit not only for the recipients of such projects. The Council also expressed their enthusiasm of a threefold benefit that could arise from such cooperative projects for the sake of Christian unity. Between ecclesial communities, the Council spoke of the way such projects could lead to "understand[ing] each other better and esteem[ing] each other more," while at the same time vividly expressing to the non-Christian

---

1. *Unitatis Redintegratio* (hereinafter *UR*), 12. References to documents of the Second Vatican Council are drawn from Flannery, *Vatican Council II*. All numbers in the references to conciliar documents refer to the paragraph number(s) of those documents.

world "that bond which in fact already unites [Christians], and finally "set[ting into] clearer relief the features of Christ the Servant."[2]

While the above statements of the Council Fathers may have been promulgated more than forty years ago, the enthusiasm with the approach that was expressed by the Council Fathers finds echoes in contemporary ecumenical practice in the protestant world, as exemplified by statements by the Lutheran World Federation, the World Communion of Reformed Churches and the World Council of Churches.[3] Indeed, such enthusiasm for what may be called the social justice approach to ecumenism ostensibly seems justified in light of what sociologists and political scientists have labelled a process of "desecularization" in which religious players enjoy a much higher profile and greater credibility in engaging in sociopolitical activity.[4] According to this line of reasoning, social justice projects as corporeal works of mercy could be a legitimate avenue whereby the Christian Gospel *as an explicitly Christian Gospel* can be unequivocally proclaimed as a form of reasoning for common social action, and whereby a firm foundation on which visible ecclesial unity can be nurtured. It is here that this book wishes to intervene with a question: do such acts explicitly proclaim the Christian Gospel?

The foil for this book is this statement in paragraph 12 of *Unitatis Redintegratio*: that the social justice approach ecumenism can lead to mutual understanding, demonstrate the commonalities between Christians and forcefully proclaims Christ to the world. The concern here is not so much the legitimacy of a common witness to the poor, but whether the current practice of ministering to the poor in light of its contemporary sociopolitical context so readily communicates Christ and builds the bonds of unity between ecclesial communities.

2. Ibid.

3. For key paragraphs of these texts as well as a more detailed analysis, see Ballor, *Ecumenical Babel*.

4. Johnston and Sampson, *Religion*; Sampson, *Faith Based Diplomacy*; Thomas, *Global Resurgence of Religion*; Petito and Hatzopoulos, *Religion in International Relations*; Juergensmeyer, *New Cold War?*

Introduction

This should be a particular concern since the "desecularized" context that underpins the contemporary hope for ecumenism is also driven and mediated by the forces of media and market.[5] The fact that joint works of mercy seem justified or affirmed in the public eye when it comes in commercialized packaging points to a problem not so much in the relationship between one church and another. It seems that a more fundamental puzzle would concern the relationship between the Church and secular culture. More specifically, the fulcrum of this puzzle is located in the way in which the Church interprets culture. This is because a nexus of theological, political and cultural assumptions operate behind *Unitatis Redintegratio's* enthusiastic endorsement of the social justice approach to ecumenism, and paragraph 12 can be said to be read within the framework of a theopolitical complex.

More specifically, paragraph 12 appears to be set within the paradigm of religion entering the "public square," now called "civil society." This in turn assumes that the Church has entered a social space that is free from any cultural, religious, political or social bias, and that different churches can unproblematically engage in cooperative projects within these culturally neutral spaces. It is assumed further that due to the transparency and cultural neutrality of the public square, collaborative social justice projects undertaken by differing ecclesial communities can unequivocally proclaim Christ in common, whether between ecclesial communities or between Christians and non-Christians.

This book seeks to provide a corrective to these assumption by focussing attention on the cultural context within which such projects are implemented, particularly in a contemporary context where society is circumscribed by the state and market. This is a context that the Council Fathers may have been too hasty in baptizing. This book will argue with Henri de Lubac, contrary to the assumption ostensibly adopted by the Council Fathers that the public square was a culturally neutral sphere, that all social spaces bear within them some cultural agenda.[6] The cultural agenda operating within these

---

5. Ward, *True Religion*, vii.
6. Lubac, *Brief Catechesis on Nature and Grace*, 92.

social spaces possesses the capacity to refract the cultural logic of any given practice carried out within them. As such, the ecclesial granting of autonomy to the secular has allowed Christian witness to be culturally outflanked by the secular sphere. In other words, practices that supposedly aim to declare the message of the Servant King can be made to proclaim something rather different when set against the backdrop of the state, civil society and market. What could have been the Christian cultural logic operating within acts of social justice can be reinterpreted and geared towards non-Christian or even anti-Christian ends.

What is more, this book argues that the cultural context's refraction of the interpretation of the act of social justice is a phenomenon that will impact not only the observer of that act, but also the person that carries out that act. This means that for Christian practitioner and non-Christian observer alike, the act's Christian content, marked by the building of communion between man and God, can give way to that of political liberalism, marked by radical individualism, fragmentation and pure immanence. In light of this, it would be difficult to share today in the Council Fathers' enthusiasm for the unquestionable promise of acts of social justice for the building of communion among the Churches as articulated in paragraph 12 of *Unitatis Redintegratio*.

It must be stated at the outset that the Council Fathers were correct in looking at social justice as a potential resource for fostering Christian unity, since it can be a resource for the building of communion among differing ecclesial communities. However, it must also be stated that the Council Fathers were too hasty in regarding the surrounding culture as a merely passive category, infinitely malleable to the "development by the work of [human] hands"[7] and completely subject to the assertion of human will. At another level, it must be shown that the Council Fathers were also too hasty in baptizing the developments within modern culture as "provid[ing] some preparation for the acceptance of the message

---

7. For the full text of *Gaudium et Spes* (hereinafter *GS*), see Flannery, *Vatican Council II*, 163–282.

of the Gospel."[8] Such assumptions created a problem in cultural hermeneutics insofar as they led the Council to consider acts of social justice in themselves as clearly Christian acts regardless of the cultural context in which these acts took place. This created the outcome of the Church's being outflanked by secular culture, and allowing a de-Christianizing of the act of social justice. Resisting the de-Christianization of the act requires the Church to consider the building of a distinctly Christian cultural context within which the Christian confessions within individual acts of justice would be unmistakable.

Thus, while this analysis on its face is looking at the relationship between social justice and ecumenism, it is at the same time exploring the issue of a Christian interpretation of culture. Ultimately, as this book hopes to demonstrate, the fundamental issue is one of Christian formation. All of these categories do not occur in cultural or social vacuums, but are instead caught up in and also shaped by secular contextual factors that many assume to be neutral. In other words, awareness of a culture's meaning comes from an awareness of its theopolitical complex.

Structure of the Book

Substantiating this work's central hypothesis would be carried out in four parts. In the first part, the book will briefly outline how the Council's approach to the Christianizing of the modern world was underpinned by the Council's conception of its modern cultural surroundings as an autonomous and neutral blank slate which could be unproblematically taken up and baptized by Christian values. This section will look at the how this mindset that sustained such a belief was set within the context of the Mystical Body ecclesiology that was first framed by Jacques Maritain, an ecclesiology which split the temporal and spiritual spheres into two distinct and virtually independent zones of operation. That section will also consider how this temporal/spiritual divide informed the thought

8. Ibid.

Justice, Unity, and the Hidden Christ

of John XXIII and Paul VI, the popes who were responsible for initiating and steering the Second Vatican Council, as well as influenced Conciliar thinking in general. It will do so with reference to the document most relevant for this analysis, namely *Unitatis Redintegratio* and also look at a number of the foundational ecclesiological and pastoral statements that foregrounded the Council's self-conception with respect to the modern world and the mode of the Church's engagement with it.

Chapter 2 will critically evaluate the continued applicability of the complex of presumptions implicitly adopted by the Council Fathers in light of our contemporary postmodern context. This chapter will confine its analysis to four key presumptions. These concern the Conciliar adoption of the Cartesian subject, the presumption of the neutrality of the institutional form of any act, that of a single act bearing a clear *telos*, and the neutrality of the civil society in which the Council imagined the Church to operate. This section will show that, contrary to the assumptions entertained by the Council, the act of the Christian agent simultaneously participates in an array of non-ecclesial practices. Each set of practices is responsible in producing a social universe that Charles Taylor calls a "social imaginary," which sets the cultural logic and horizons of the agent participating in such practices.[9] Because of the profound intermingling of agents within multiple practices and thus multiple imaginaries at any one time, the endless production and reproduction of interlocking social imaginaries unavoidably implicates Christians in what Graham Ward calls "the politics of belief."[10] Christian action is thus bound up in and conditioned by the interlocking of Christian discourses with non-Christian ones, as well as the Church's positioning of itself vis-à-vis non-Christian configurations. As such, the explicitly Christian confessions of any practice, including any act of social justice, may become obscured and even refracted in a predominantly secular cultural environment. Thus, a secular social structure can powerfully refract any act towards ends other than the one intended by the Christian

9. C. Taylor, *Modern Social Imaginaries*.
10. Ward, *Cities of God*, 212.

agent. This means that the practice of social justice may not in and of itself yield sufficient shared Christian cultural data from which to build greater unity among ecclesial communities in the way envisioned by the Council Fathers in *Unitatis Redintegratio*.

Chapter 3 would dedicate itself to assessing just how Christian the cultural presumptions of the contemporary cultural context are. It will argue that in light of a social context dominated by the state and market, and in light of a self-conception of the Church as a specialist in its own spiritual sphere of operations, the Church's political horizons and modes of action have become subordinated to the logic of the state/society/market complex. The Church is seen to play what Michael Budde and Robert Brimlow call a chaplaincy role to this dominant capitalist order.[11] This leads to the Church playing second fiddle in determining the ends of the individual act of social justice, which in turn leads to two interconnecting outcomes inimical to ecumenism. First, insofar as the Church refracts its theology through the lens of the state/society/market complex, the Church will fail to steer its acts of social justice to their Christic end, since they have become displaced by the ends of secular modernity. Second, insofar as that act of social justice has the ends of secular modernity as its *telos*, the Christian content within the act itself would become obscured by that secular *telos*. Thus, ecumenism as the building of communion among ecclesial communities becomes undermined by a project emphasizing atomism, struggle and productivity.

Chapter 4 would briefly consider how, if the evaluation of the Council Fathers' positioning of the Church vis-à-vis secular culture is correct, and if that positioning is also inimical to both Christian mission and visible ecclesial unity, then the Body of Christ ought to resituate itself vis-à-vis its secular counterparts. If the ecclesiology of the Church as chaplain to the capitalist order has relegated the Body of Christ to merely a subsection of a public circumscribed the state/society/market complex, then the Body of Christ ought to be repositioned to become a public in its own right, whilst at the same time avoiding a replication of the very

11. Budde and Brimlow, *Christianity Incorporated*.

secular logic that the Church seeks to critique. This book will look at sacramental practice, and pay special attention to eucharistic liturgical practice, as this distinctly ecclesial mode of action that can nurture this distinctly Christian public space within which a particular act, including an act of social justice, could have its ends shaped by a distinctly Christian *telos*. It will conclude by briefly considering some of areas where the linking of the act of social justice to the cultural logic of the Eucharist could provide a corrective to when that same act of social justice is tied to the state/society/market complex.

CHAPTER 1

Unitatis Redintegratio and Vatican II's Engagement with Secular Culture

Introduction

LOOKING AT THE TEXT of *Unitatis Redintegratio* in isolation would not yield the observations concerning the ease by which the Council Fathers presumed the neutrality of culture. However, such presumptions do become apparent when *Unitatis Redintegratio* is set within the larger Conciliar project of *aggiornamento,* which is outlined in the Council's Pastoral Constitution on the Church in the modern world, namely *Gaudium et Spes.*

This chapter would focus on identifying the drivers of this Conciliar attitude to culture. It will first consider how the theological context was set by Jacques Maritain's splitting of the spiritual and temporal spheres into two virtually independent entities, and his emphasis on the autonomy of the temporal sphere. It will then demonstrate the continuation of his influence in the thought of both Pope John XXIII and Paul VI, before demonstrating the continuation of his themes as eventually crystallised in *Gaudium et Spes,* which has been a powerful influence in shaping the Church's orientation to the modern world.

Justice, Unity, and the Hidden Christ

The Approach to Culture in the Lead-up to the Council

The Mystical Body and the Divine/Temporal Split

It is important to note how the Council was foregrounded by the influence of the ecclesiology of the Mystical Body, in particular the variety as articulated by Jacques Maritain. Although this was never what Maritain actually called his ecclesial vision, it nevertheless underpinned much of the thinking on the Mystical Body. Mystical Body ecclesiology grew out of a wave of what Robert Krieg calls "reform Catholicism" among scholars and pastoral leaders, who called for an ecclesial breaking out of its own self-imposed confines and renewal of what were deemed outdated practices and institutions, and reach out to a Europe that was psychically jaded by the ravages of the First World War.[1] It was within this milieu that Jacques Maritain rose to prominence within Catholic scholarship. Maritain had demonstrated his capabilities as one of the most innovative Thomists alive in twentieth century Europe. Not only was his grasp of traditional Thomistic categories unrivalled by his contemporaries, but as Paul Sigmund notes, Maritain also had the uncanny ability to use "traditional Thomistic categories to argue to a conclusion that would have horrified Saint Thomas."[2] This innovation was important because Maritain was able to accord to Catholic philosophy contemporary currency through his near seamless integration of thirteenth century Catholic theology with twentieth century social trends.[3]

Key among his innovations is his modern articulation of the neo-scholastic position on the relationship between nature and supernature. In *Integral Humanism*, Maritain wrote that man sought two "absolutely ultimate ends," a purely natural goal of seeking "perfect prosperity" and another purely supernatural goal that sought "perfect beatitude in heaven." Maritain was critical of modernity in its insistence on a sharp separation between the natural

---

1. Krieg, *Catholic Theologians in Nazi Germany*.
2. Sigmund, "Maritain on Politics," 161.
3. Schall, *Jacques Maritain*, xi–xii.

and the supernatural, which led to a "mechanical dichotomy" that split man into two distinct beings. He argued that whilst having legitimate temporal ends, temporality was still subject to the natural law, which made the temporal sphere unavoidably oriented towards God.[4] There was thus an "organic subordination" of the natural to the supernatural into a cohesive whole.[5] The correct conception of the relationship between nature and supernature for Maritain thus lay in joining two "movements," where the "horizontal" historical movement of man can only be understood by reference to a "vertical" movement towards eternal life.[6]

Nevertheless, Maritain's antipathy to the Enlightenment was not complete. While Maritain saw modernity's dichotomizing nature and supernature as harmful, he also saw great benefits in the secularisation that came with the Enlightenment. Maritain was critical of medieval Christendom's failure to fully grasp the Gospel message, the defining hallmark of which was freedom.[7] This translated into history as the legitimate human goal of self-mastery and autonomy from coercive forces that compelled man only to pursue aspirations that were antithetical to his own.[8] More specifically, Maritain was critical of the instrumentalization of the natural to the complete service of the supernatural (institutionalised in medieval Christendom), as if the natural had no proper purpose of its own. Maritain argued that whilst nature had to be subordinated to supernatural ends, the natural sphere still had relatively ultimate ends of its own that could be legitimately pursued independently of the supernatural ends.[9] Maritain thus affirmed the Enlightenment's creation of a sphere of freedom for the secular to operate free from the illegitimate confinement of the supernatural, the "autonomy of the temporal as an intermediate or infravalent end."[10]

4. Maritain, *Religion and Culture*, 5–8.
5. Maritain, *Integral Humanism*, 22.
6. Maritain, "Integral Humanism," 1–17.
7. Sigmund, "Maritain on Politics," 157.
8. Maritain, *On the Philosophy of History*, 125.
9. Ibid., 130–32.
10. Maritain, *Integral Humanism*, 176–77.

Justice, Unity, and the Hidden Christ

This affirmation of the autonomy of legitimate secular ends, however, did not mean a fundamental separation between nature and supernature. The latter still indirectly (and non-coercively) related to the former. Rather than instrumentalizing the secular, Maritain argued that the supernatural properly subordinated nature by "vivify[ing] to its most intimate depths the order of... the temporal."[11] The supernatural no longer coerced nature because it operated within the structures of nature. There was thus an effective bifurcation of the divine and temporal into two separate spheres, which underpinned Maritain's ecclesiological reconceptualization of Christendom. As Maritain would later declare in 1930, this was the underpinning for the realisation of a "New Christendom" where "the spiritual and moral action of the Church presides over a temporal order."[12] In his *Primacy of the Supernatural* (published in English under the title *Things that are Not Caesar's*),[13] Maritain cemented New Christendom's place as the foundation of ecclesial politics for many decades to come. Maritain took Christ's famous instruction to "render unto Caesar what belongs to Caesar, and to God what belongs to God" to be a Christ-given mandate for the separation between the spiritual and political spheres and the proper autonomy of one from the other. By giving this instruction, Christ was supposed to have "distinguished the two powers and in so doing emancipated the souls of men."[14]

According to Maritain, spiritual and temporal powers operated legitimately in two distinct realms. The temporal realm could be part of the unfolding of God's revelation in accordance with the laws of that sphere. More importantly, nature and supernature in Maritain's view could properly operate autonomously from each other, and so the temporal realm could be conceived as being part of the unfolding of Divine revelation even when it operated autonomously from the supernatural realm. As to the question of authority proper to each realm, Maritain regarded the Church as

11. Ibid., 176.
12. Amato, *Mounier and Maritain*, 107.
13. Maritain, *The Things That Are Not Caesar's*.
14. Ibid., 2.

the proper ultimate authority in the spiritual realm, "the province of faith and morals [and] of salvation."[15] The authority to directly govern political things in the temporal realm lay with the state. For Maritain, Aquinas' conception of temporal authority seamlessly flowed into the modern State. Despite his critiques of modernity, Maritain seemed to regard the modern state as "the most perfect natural community . . . which mankind can form in this world,"[16] since it epitomized the proper differentiation of the temporal from the spiritual.

That being said, the state was not fully autonomous from the church, since temporal realm was not *fully* autonomous from the spiritual. For Maritain, man is "ordered directly to God as to his eternal end" and only the Church as the proper hegemon of the spiritual realm could lay any such claims to ultimacy.[17] The temporal realm is thus not fully independent of the spiritual, since a Maritainian humanism requires the former in order to find meaning in the latter. Whilst the political realm is rightfully autonomous within its own sphere, it is subordinate to the spiritual realm in matters of ultimate meaning.[18] The Church thus intervenes in politics through the injection of a base of values that indirectly Christianizes any action taken in the temporal realm, even if that action may not be seen to be particularly Christian.

The Mystical Body Immediately Before the Council

Although Maritain is credited with shaping ecclesial politics of the pre- and wartime papacies, one must note the continuing influence on ecclesial political thought that lasted up to the late 1970s.[19] For

15. Ibid., 7.
16. Ibid., 2.
17. Ibid., 4.
18. Ibid., 14.
19. As an example, William Cavanaugh and Daniel Bell cite the continuing influence of Jacques Maritain on the thought of theologians of liberation in South America. See Cavanaugh, *Torture and Eucharist*, 178; Bell Jr., *Liberation Theology*, 45–64.

the purposes of this book, it is important only to note the continuing influence of Maritain in the immediate pre-Conciliar period. This is to aid understanding of the assumptions that circumscribed the drafting of references to ecclesial social action, in particular social action as a step to Christian unity as outlined in paragraph 12 of *Unitatis Redintegratio*.

As an aside, it must be noted that Maritain's position on the relationship between the divine and the temporal was not the only one that was taken up in the Council, although the trajectory of thought of these other writers is strikingly similar (this is indicative of the degree of his influence in ecclesiological thought). For instance, in an article in the first edition of *Concilium*, Edward Schillebeeckx argued for a dialectical relationship between the Church on the one hand and mankind on the other. Schillebeeckx criticised the sectarian and obsessively otherworldly orientation of the pre-Conciliar Church, in a manner that did not take temporal affairs seriously, and abandoned the authentic building of a community of persons.[20] Instead of adopting Maritain's notion of a spiritual sphere that is distinct from the temporal, Schillebeeckx spoke of the salvific work of unifying mankind through "the fraternal service of one chosen from among ourselves—Jesus Christ." God's plan of salvation thus "took place in our history and in our secular and human affairs." This meant that mankind's real unity rests upon the agency of God's saving will concretely within history, and the Church thus actualises this as a concrete reality.[21]

However, despite Schillebeeckx's starting point of a more historically oriented focus on the saving work of God, it is striking how similar Schillebeeckx's conclusions are to Maritain's. One must consider Schillebeeckx's first assertion that in Christ, immanence becomes an extension of transcendence.[22] He spoke of a "fluidity of the boundaries between the Church and mankind." In a latter part of the essay, he spoke of creation being "a divine act that

---

20. Schillebeeckx, "Church and Mankind," 42.
21. Ibid., 36–37.
22. Ibid., 42.

Unitatis Redintegratio *and Vatican II's Engagement*

situates realities within their respective spheres."[23] Schillebeeckx also drew on Scripture to argue that as part of the divine act of creation, "mankind will assert itself as the progressive and prolonged desacralization of earthly structures and functions." The growing independence of the world from the Church thus became not a bifurcation into the sacred and profane, but the beginnings of a dialectic between "two complementary, authentically Christian expressions of the same God-related life concealed in the mystery of Christ."[24] Where once there was a specialised function for the Church, desacralization has led to an "osmosis from the Church to the world,"[25] so much so that the holiness of the Church can become tested "by the authenticity of our fellowship," the standards of which can be derived from "words, concepts and pictures taken from our human environment."[26] The secular could thus be said to set the standards of what is sacred. Though beginning with the rejection of Maritain's quarantining of the Church from the secular world, in an indirect fashion, Schillebeeckx appears to affirm Maritain's assertion that the secular has a proper autonomy that the Church must respect when carrying out its mission.

To return to the legacy of Maritain's influence on pre-Conciliar thought, consideration must first be given to Pope John XXIII, the pope responsible for calling the council in the first place. While it is well known that John XXIII called the Council with a view to update the Church, it is the terms by which he sought such an updating that are of interest, and one must note how John XXIII's program to engage the Church with the modern world was framed by Maritain's ecclesiological reflections. The first sign of this can be found in one of his key encyclicals, *Mater et Magistra*.[27] In it, Pope John XXIII explicitly reminded Catholics that they are members of a Body of Christ whose configuration was mystical.[28] The conti-

---

23. Ibid., 41.
24. Ibid.
25. Ibid., 44.
26. Ibid., 48–49.
27. John XXIII, *Mater et Magistra* (hereinafter *MM*).
28. Ibid., 159.

nuities between the Mystical Body and "New Christendom" ecclesiology can be seen despite the differences in name. For example, in *Mater et Magistra*, Christians were indeed called to reverse the devastation of the war and "improve their own temporal institutions and environment."[29] However, he reminded Catholics that they could only do so in a manner that continued Maritain's respect for the autonomy of the temporal. Indeed, as he would later write in *Pacem in Terris*,[30] some key developments within the modern world, such as the pursuit of human rights, could be seen as part of mankind's "homage to God"[31] and even part of a *"preparatio evangelii,"* even when they were pursued outside the visible confines of the Church. The pope afforded no temporal competence to the Church and enjoined Catholics to corporeally act "in accordance with the laws . . . which correspond to their respective natures."[32] Thus, if Catholics became temporally involved *as Catholics*, they had to do so by individually reorienting their intentions and hearts and fulfil their "duty to carry on their economic and social activities in a Christian manner,"[33] bringing only "Christian motives and a Christian spirit" to "slightly affect" the temporal world.[34] At the same time, the form by which all their actions took had to be moulded in accordance with the laws of the temporal realm.

The need for Christians to adapt the contours of what constitutes Christian action in accordance to the laws of the temporal sphere is further articulated in the writings of the pope who would steer the final stages of the Council, Paul VI. This can be seen from his first encyclical, *Ecclesiam Suam*.[35] The document did not intend to be a coherent instruction on ecclesiology, but a set of guidelines for the deliberations of the then ongoing Second Vatican Council. Still, the document is significant for its reflecting

29. Ibid., 179.
30. John XXIII, *Pacem in Terris* (hereinafter *PT*).
31. Ibid., 50.
32. Ibid., 150.
33. *MM.*, 228.
34. *PT*, 151.
35. Paul VI, *Ecclesiam Suam* (hereinafter *ES*).

several important ecclesiological elements articulated by Paul's predecessors that would prove influential in the Council. One of the most telling themes was the assertion by Paul VI that the Church's mission had to "adapt itself to the forms of thought and living which a temporal environment induces, one might almost say imposes." Because of this imposition, the Church had to undergo "a continual process of self-examination and re-appraisal of its external conduct."[36] Thus for Paul, the Church in carrying out its mission to "make the world share in the divine redemption," also had to "approach [the world] with *reverence* . . . and love,"[37] so that "the world, and . . . the Catholic Church . . . should meet together and get to know and love one another."[38] In keeping with the temporal/spiritual split enjoined by Maritain, Paul wrote that the Church's temporal role lay in "proclaim[ing] principles which represent the highest achievement of human thought." Any more involved a function could only be undertaken when the Church is "allowed the opportunity" by those in charge of the temporal sphere.[39]

The Mystical Body and the Conciliar Approach to Culture

The above reflections may be those of two individuals, but it is important to note that the influence of Maritain's thought extended far beyond these two popes. It is also important to note that the ecclesiological horizons articulated by these two popes are indicative of a set of presumptions concerning the modern world that a sizeable proportion of the Council fathers brought to the Council, judging by the articulations set within *Gaudium et Spes*.[40]

---

36. Ibid., 42.
37. Ibid., 69.
38. Ibid., 3.
39. Ibid., 16.
40. Langan, "Political Hopes, Political Tasks," 102; *Gaudium et Spes*, 57.

Justice, Unity, and the Hidden Christ

In the articulation of the Church's engagement with modern culture, several things become apparent. As Tracey Rowland argued in her analysis of the Council, no coherent concept of culture was provided by the Council in the first place.[41] The Council Fathers acknowledged that culture was a multifaceted category, defining it as "all those things which go to the refining and development of humanity's diverse mental and physical endowments." Such a definition is open to a slew of interpretations and reference points, from the pursuit of human rights, the scientific advancements that gave the world the pill and the atom bomb, to the ascendency of liberal democracy, to work, or to the Beatles.[42] Yet, no criterion seemed to be utilised by the Council Fathers to delineate the subject of their consideration—culture—at the Council.

There thus seemed to be an impression at the Council that there was a ready availability of meaning within this subject called "culture." It must be noted that, set against the backdrop of the ascendency of scientific empiricism in which all values are readily scrutable in an objective sense, mid-twentieth century social analysis did not discern the need to engage in an interpretation of what was yielded via subjective cultural categories. In other words, there was an impression that the data yielded by observing these cultural categories were self-explanatory, universally accessible and thus universally valid regardless of the social or cultural context within which the observer was situated. If culture did not factor as a variable for analysis, it was deemed irrelevant as far as the horizons of any analysis were concerned. Little surprise then, that when it came to the need to interface the church with modern culture there was, as John O'Malley noted, little awareness within the Council of the need to furnish a "consistent theoretical foundation" of its own that could furnish the Church with a guide for such a cultural engagement.[43]

According to Rowland, this lack of a "consistent theoretical foundation" created a hermeneutical problem as far as the central

---

41. Rowland, *Culture and the Thomist Tradition*, 17–19.
42. Ibid., 20.
43. O'Malley, *Tradition and Transition*, 45.

theme of the Second Vatican Council—*aggiornamento*—was concerned. The specific problem Rowland identified was a lack of a coherent standard outside the modern world by which the contours and direction of the Church's *aggiornamento* could be discerned.[44] As with "culture," the concept of *aggiornamento* was not a self-explanatory term and is tied with multiple meanings, the application of each of which could take the church in different directions. This problematic was summed up by a question Karl Barth put to Paul VI after the council: what does *aggiornamento* mean? Accommodation to what?[45] As this question reveals, one of the implicit elements within the concept of *aggiornamento* was the application of some kind of criterion that the Church had to meet in order to determine the success of its updating and adaptation. The use of an *external* standard is important to note here since, as was mentioned earlier, the Church came with no coherent theoretical foundation of its own in seeking to engage modern culture. This leads to the question: what did the Council use as its external standard in its deliberations on the modern world?

Walter Kasper, commenting on the driving forces behind *Gaudium et Spes*, noted that there was a strong desire among the Council Fathers to reject in explicit terms the idea that the Church can "provide the answer to secular questions directly from the faith."[46] The unarticulated catch cry within the Council, according to Kasper, was that "secular matters are to be decided in a secular fashion" and that no secular issue was to be considered "magisterially or theologically," that is, with recourse to sources that would properly be called ecclesial or Christian.[47] As Rowland observed, in the absence of providing a coherent external standard of its own, considering "secular matters in a secular fashion" for the Council in general and *Gaudium et Spes* in particular was ultimately, in the words of Cardinal Aloysius Ambrozic "either mainly or at least significantly an attempt to reconcile the Gospel

---

44. Rowland, *Culture and the Thomist Tradition*, 19.
45. Barth, *Ad Limina Apostolorum*, 20.
46. Kasper, *Faith and the Future*, 4.
47. Ibid.

and the Enlightenment."⁴⁸ Rowland also alludes to the reflections of Bernard Lambert, who was a conciliar *peritus* who proved influential in the final drafting of *Gaudium et Spes*. According to Lambert, the task of the document was to proclaim and embrace the notion of the now famous catchphrase, "the autonomy of the secular."⁴⁹ According to this concept, a secular sphere existed that had quite legitimately "free[d] itself from religious notions, beliefs or institutions which used to order its existence" and "now [was] constituted as an autonomous society . . . [with] its own consistency, methods, structures and laws for its own organisation."⁵⁰ It is instructive to consider the overlaps between the type of *aggiornamento* embodied in these observations and the influence on the Council by Maritain's respect for the legitimate autonomy of the temporal sphere. In other words, the external standard that was adopted in the Church's engagement with the modern world was the modern world itself, or more specifically the logic that operated within modern culture.

The content of that modern cultural logic will be elaborated in a later section. For now, one needs to consider the evidence of the Church's deference to the secular within the Conciliar documents themselves. In the dogmatic constitution of the Church, *Lumen Gentium*,⁵¹ the Council Fathers framed their affirmation of the Church as the "light of the world" within the confines of another affirmation: that "the temporal sphere is governed by its own principles."⁵² This is an implicit statement as to the Church's own competences in secular matters, or more precisely, the lack thereof. What is implied in that statement is made more explicit in several places in *Gaudium et Spes*, the document that best indicated the mind of the Church on the very issue of the Church's engagement with modern culture. Paragraph 44 of *Gaudium et Spes* is

48. Cited in Rowland, *Culture and the Thomist Tradition*, 29.
49. Ibid.
50. Cited in Ibid.
51. The full text of *Lumen Gentium* (hereinafter *LG*) can be found in Flannery, *Vatican Council II*, 97–116.
52. *LG*, 36.

particularly revealing here, for it builds on *Lumen Gentium*'s statements on the autonomy of the temporal sphere as well as make more explicit the implied lack of the Church's competence in secular matters. These observations are encapsulated in the approach of "accommodated preaching of the revealed word."[53] While the word "accommodated" taken in isolation might seem a bit vague, the terms of that accommodation start to become clearer when the continued influence of Maritain's split of the autonomous temporal and divine sphere is considered together with the above extra-documentary comments by those most intimately involved in the Conciliar process. The Church had to subordinate itself to the secular world when determining the content of its *aggiornamento*. The need for an external, secular standard for the Church can be further justified in a number of sections of *Gaudium et Spes* itself.

On this score, paragraphs 34, 36 and 44 are particularly revealing. In paragraph 34, in relation to man's activity in the world, the Council Fathers mentioned that the mandate given to man by God in the first chapter of the Book of Genesis—to exercise dominion over the earth—meant that works of rational man were not set in opposition to the divine creator of man. Rather, because man is made in the image of God, man's activity in the world always participates in the unfolding of God's will on earth. "The triumphs of the human race," therefore, "are a sign of God's grace and the flowering of His mysterious design."[54] However, the unfolding of God's design in this manner only came about through the recognition of "an autonomy of earthly affairs," which is the "gradual discovery, utilization and ordering of the laws and values of matter and society."[55] It spoke of the Church's being enriched "by the history and development of humankind." This meant more than a mere augmenting of what the Church already has for the world. In the eyes of the Council, the Church's engagement with the world actually "depend[ed] on things outside itself" and required the particular assistance of "its individual sons and daughters ... [and]

---

53. *GS*, 44.
54. Ibid., 34.
55. Ibid., 36.

by people of all classes and conditions," who "contribute[d] to the development of the human community on the level of family, culture, economic and social life."[56] The Council Fathers even went as far to say that the Church "greatly benefited and is still benefiting from the opposition its enemies and persecutors" since "whoever promotes the human community . . . according to God's design, is also contributing in no small way to the community of the Church."[57]

It must be noted that the Council's openness to the world as expressed in paragraph 44 was not unqualified, for in the following paragraph the Council spoke of the continuing need of creation for God,[58] and the Council's awareness of the centrality of bringing God's Kingdom to pass.[59] Nevertheless, it is interesting how the mode of the coming of God's Kingdom, and the Church's place in that process, continues to show the influence of Maritain's split of the temporal and divine spheres. On the one hand, the Church had to cede expertise to those who lived in the world, since the world had a rightful autonomy from religion as far as its institutional governance was concerned. On the other hand, the role of the church in unfolding God's designs within creation seems to be an indirect one, one that repeats Maritain's model of the spiritual vivifying of the temporal order, infusing the right values into practices even as they are governed by processes that are rightly autonomous from religious instruction.

The influence of Maritain's thought on this score is encapsulated in the Conciliar desire to "assess by that light those values which are most highly prized . . . and to relate them to their divine source."[60] In spite of the many changes that are embodied in modern culture, and in spite of their affirmation that such changes participate in the unfolding of God's grace within creation, the Council still spoke of the Church's important role in linking these

56. Ibid., 44.
57. Ibid.
58. Ibid., 36.
59. Ibid., 45.
60. Ibid., 11.

institutional changes back to their "ultimate foundation in Christ, Who is the same yesterday and yesterday, and today, and forever."[61] The problem that arises at this point is that, having affirmed the institutional shape of cultural changes as goods in themselves, the only avenue whereby the Church could engage the world was through an internal "purification" via the realm of values. The site of action for the Church in the engagement with the modern world thus was where these values are situated. For the Council Fathers then, as it was for Maritain, the Church should not engage in any interference with the institutional operations of secular culture due to their rightful autonomy from the Church. Where the Church *could* properly intervene was in the *hearts* of those who participated in secular culture.

The cornerstone of the Council's approach can be found in paragraph 12 of *Gaudium et Spes*, which posited the human subject as the "centre and summit" of all things on earth. This paragraph betrays a subjectivist turn that made human subjectivity the central concern, or as the Council put it, "the true state of humanity . . . its dignity and vocation."[62] Because of sin, the human situation has become distorted, and this distortion takes place through an upsetting of the proper order of values, even while the institutional arrangements within secular culture remain goods in themselves.[63] This for the Council constituted the anatomy of the social ills that plagued its contemporary context. The Church's salvific mission for the world thus lay not in changing the institutions themselves, but in enriching and perfecting them with a vague category known as "heavenly benefits."[64] All enterprises are thus "integrate[d] . . . with religious values, under whose supreme direction all things are ordered to the glory of God."[65] But exactly how these "values" come to perfect them remained ill defined.

61. Ibid., 10.
62. Ibid., 12.
63. Ibid., 37.
64. Ibid., 40.
65. Ibid., 43.

Conclusion: *Unitatis Redintegratio* in Light of *Aggiornamento*

The sections above first briefly considered the Maritain's autonomization of the temporal from the spiritual and the indirect subordination of the former by the latter. It then considered how, in both post-war papal and Conciliar thought, this curious mix of autonomy combined with indirect subordination played itself out in both *Lumen Gentium* and *Gaudium et Spes*. Without abandoning the need for bringing the Christian Gospel to the world, the Council Fathers thought that this had to be done with the recognition that the Gospel should have no impact on the institutional makeup of secular cultural forms, lest the principle of the "autonomy of culture" is violated. Instead, extra-Conciliar commentary and the wording of the documents themselves point to an approach whereby the Church was a deposit of values that worked mysteriously on the hearts of those who engaged in the practices of secular culture. In doing so, the Church fulfilled its evangelical role by invisibly tying in the temporal realm to the proper order of values.

In this concluding section, attention must now be given to the pastoral application of the principles articulated above in relation to the social justice approach as articulated in paragraph 12 of *Unitatis Redintegratio*. While the social justice approach to ecumenism continued Maritain's splitting of the temporal and spiritual spheres, it faces one major conceptual hurdle: the concept of the "autonomy of culture" is absent in the text of Paragraph 12. The fact that the Conciliar respect for the "autonomy of culture" is not explicitly mentioned within the document itself may present a problem in substantiating this book's case. However, if the horizons of the ecumenical task of the Church are set by the task of bringing the Gospel to the world, as is explicitly stated in paragraph 1 of *Unitatis Redintegratio*, then it would be reasonable to assume that the social justice approach to ecumenism expressed in paragraph 12 should similarly be read within the context of the Church's self-conception vis-à-vis the world as articulated in *Lumen Gentium* and *Gaudium et Spes*. As it is, the phrasing of this paragraph seemed to indicate that no deviation of the Conciliar respect for the "autonomy of culture" was intended as the Council affirmed social justice as a privileged mode of action by which a common witness to Christ could be made.

It is argued that this comes out in a distinction between engaging in a mode of social action, which are governed by "social and technological evolution" and the infusing of a Christian "values" in those actions. Whilst the Council strongly encouraged the use of "every possible means to relieve the afflictions of our times," this seemed to be distinct from a mode of action which is explicitly ecclesial. In the two instances where the Church's distinctly Christian contribution can be made in carrying out social justice, their role seemed to be limited to the infusion of a "Christian spirit."[66] Importantly, this did not stop their participation in carrying out acts of social justice *per se*. However, were the Church to engage in those actions, the shape of those actions had to be properly framed by technical categories determined by the secular sphere. Critique of these technical categories stood outside the Church sphere of competence. Therefore, it would seem imperative that were the Church to engage the modern world, the physical shape of the Church's actions had to conform to the standards set by secular institutions. The brevity of paragraph 12 means that the weight of explicit evidence for this assertion would not be as great as the wealth of evidence found in relation to *Gaudium et Spes*. Nevertheless, the centrality role of *Gaudium et Spes* in orienting the Church to the modern world, the intentions of those that were intimately involved in the process as evinced by their commentaries, and the ecclesiological foregrounding of the Conciliar process by the popes most involved in the Conciliar process makes this hermeneutical trajectory difficult to avoid.

It is the burden of this book to show that if this is indeed the Conciliar reading of secular culture, then the Church's continued engagement via such a reading would have limited application in our contemporary context. A preliminary to this problematic can be found within the reading of the Conciliar documents

---

66. *UR*, 12.

themselves. There is a question of whether, if the temporal forms of social action are considered to be autonomous from the Church and thus contoured by a secular logic, such actions are sufficient means to identify the action as proclamations of a distinctly Christian Gospel. This seems to be articulated in a section of paragraph 12 in which actions of social justice are said to "set in clearer relief the features of Christ the Servant" because they raise the dignity of the human person.[67] Yet, if the visible aspect of an act of social justice can only be properly shaped by an autonomous secular sphere, how is it possible to discern merely from observing the phenomenon of that practice that Christ is being proclaimed? This is compounded by the fact that, as *Gaudium et Spes* itself pointed out, what actually constitutes human dignity is subject to "views that are divergent and even contradictory."[68] The act of social justice, even when seen to uphold or promote human dignity, would then similarly be subject to the same fragmentation of meaning when it becomes interpreted through different lenses. What constitutes dignity, for example, for the Christian could easily become divergent with what constitutes dignity for the liberal, because "dignity" is not a universal given. Rather, "dignity," like any trope, must be subject to some form of interpretation.[69] If this is so, then it would be difficult to reconcile the Conciliar observation on the one hand of the divergent conceptions of dignity (as articulated in *Gaudium et Spes*), and its confidence on the other about the clear correlation between the promotion of human dignity and the proclamation of Christ in the context of an act of social justice (as articulated in *Unitatis Redintegratio*). This seeming incongruity is the thin end of the conceptual wedge for the Council. Indeed, it opens up a range of problematics that would seriously qualify the Council's confidence in the social justice approach to ecumenism, which the next chapter will explore.

---

67. *UR*, 12.
68. *GS*, 12.
69. Rowland, *Culture and the Thomist Tradition*, 20.

CHAPTER 2

The Council, Its Presuppositions, and Postmodernity

Introduction

THE PREVIOUS CHAPTER CONSIDERED how the Council's notion of the autonomy of culture was shaped by the notion of splitting of the divine and temporal into two distinct spheres, and making the temporal indirectly subordinate to the spiritual. However, the temporal already participated in the unfolding of God's plan within history and thus could legitimately develop under its own governance. Its institutional shape had to remain unmolested by any intrusion from the spiritual sphere. Under such circumstances the Church at the Second Vatican Council considered itself to have no competence to directly determine the institutional shape of any social action. The Church could only accept social arrangements as they are found and could only internally vivify those arrangements through the infusion of values.

The previous chapter also argued that this approach to temporal matters, as articulated in *Gaudium et Spes*, formed the theoretical foreground for the social justice approach to ecumenism as articulated in paragraph 12 of *Unitatis Redintegratio*. This is evinced by the very wording of key sentences of the paragraph, which pointed to the Church's ceding of competence in determining the institutional shape of any social action to the governance of secular "technical evolution." This confined the Church's competence in such actions to the infusion of a "Christian spirit" while leaving intact those secular institutional forms.

In order to evaluate the claim articulated by the Council Fathers that social justice can form an adequate basis for a common proclamation of Christ that is both evangelical and nourishing for visible Church unity, it will be necessary to undertake an evaluation of the unarticulated theoretical foregrounding to such a claim. Analyzing the theopolitical complex as adopted by the Council Fathers would be the central task of this chapter and the next. The investigation in this chapter will take place in three phases. The first phase will be a brief highlighting of some of the presumptions that would have made such a Conciliar reading possible, with particular attention paid to the strong conception of the Cartesian subject, the distinction between the action and its cultural logic and the presumption of a Christian *telos* inherent within any single act in isolation. Addressing these presumptions will form the basis for the second phase of this evaluation. It will show not only how the institutional form and cultural location of an act actually determines its cultural logic, but also how the Church's allowing of the secular to determine the institutional form actually makes the Church a chaplain and buttress to a secular culture which is dominated by the state and market. The third phase of this chapter's evaluation of the Council's confidence in the social justice approach to ecumenism will highlight the cultural logic that acts of social justice proclaim when these acts are set against the backdrop of the state and market. This section will also show how this logic, characterised by atomism, fundamentally militates against the cementing of bonds between churches as radically communal ecclesial formations. Ultimately, this section will seek to explore one of the questions that is implicit in paragraph 12 of *Unitatis Redintegratio*: if Christian acts are to bring Christians from different churches together, what then constitutes a Christian act?

The Council Meets the Cartesian Agent

What feeds the credibility of the idea of the "autonomy of culture" as mentioned in the first chapter is the notion of the passivity of cultural forms. What informs this idea in turn is the strong conception of the subject as a unified, stable agent that is subject only to the exercise of one's own will. It is often argued that it is the Christian intentions of the agents that determine the distinctly Christian nature of the act of social justice, and this would be in keeping with Maritain's conception of the spiritual vivifying of the temporal act. The act can be internally Christianised by the strong agent even when its external structure remains intact. While this may be a very attractive reading of the problematic at hand, this reading assumes a very strong conception of the human subject that is autonomous, self-sufficient and self-defining, and thus is always certain as to what it knows and wants. The question must be raised here: can a Christian perspective countenance the strong Cartesian subject in the same way that the Council Fathers seem to have done?

The presumption of this kind of subjectivity is problematic in light of the discursive turn highlighted by Michel Foucault. This turn undercuts the strong Cartesian reading of cultural production presumed by the Council because agency in a Foucauldian reading does not rest with the human subject. Rather, the focus shifts from the "theory of the knowing subject" to the subject borne of "discursive practice."[1] In this reading the strong conception of the subject is undercut because the subject is no longer seen to be a static unitary center, the Cartesian ego-subject which defines itself. As Graham Ward points out, the discursive subject is not stable but always "in process," constantly being affected by the "time and spacing within which any subject position is oriented."[2] The subject according to Foucault does not form itself by the exercise of its own will. Rather it is constantly being formed by the discourses circulating in the subject's social environment. Thus when the subject is performing an act, he is simultaneously being

1. Foucault, *The Order of Things*, xiv.
2. Ward, *Cities of God*, 17.

immersed in and formed by a whole array of other practices and symbols—Charles Taylor's social imaginary mentioned in a previous chapter. This immersion of the subject within the discourses of these imaginaries play a central role in forming the subject's conceptions of himself and his world, and this conception of self and world is not a static and unitary category but is multiple and disperse.[3] This means that the subject is fragmented and constantly being changed as the contours of an imaginary changes. The subject would be "unstable . . . [with no] immediate consciousness of itself"[4] and this would militate against the conception of the static unitary subject presumed by the Council.

The implicit Conciliar acceptance of the Cartesian subject is problematic even from a theological perspective. This problematic is highlighted by Graham Ward's instructive exploration into Christian agency in a Christian act. Ward identifies six elements of a Christian action, the first of which is the agent.[5] Contra the notion of the fully rational Cartesian agent, Ward argues that Christian thought in the tradition of Augustine's *Confessions* had assumed agents to remain unknown even to their own inner spirits.[6] Coupling this with Augustine's notion of the Christian's earthly sojourn towards the heavenly city, Ward spoke of agency as intimately tied to a process of migration.[7] In the same way that the Foucauldian subject is "in process," the Christian agent as a citizen of the heavenly city is always a stranger and pilgrim in the earthly city.[8] According to Ward, Christian agents are constantly acquiring their identity as subjects "as they act and are acted upon in the reciprocities of relation to God and others."[9] Because of this, the Christian agent can only act from a position of incompleteness of knowledge, even if it is not a complete ignorance. This applies not

---

3. Ward, "Postmodern Theology," 325.
4. Ward, *Cities of God*, 17.
5. Ward, "Christian Act," 31.
6. Ibid., 36.
7. Ibid.
8. Heb 11:13–16
9. Webster, "Human Person," 227.

only to the world around the Christian agent, but also, if Ward's take on Augustine is taken seriously, the Christian agent itself.[10]

If Ward is critical of the strong notion of subjectivity on the level of staticity, which the Council implicitly adopted, he would also be critiquing it on the level of autonomy and self-sufficiency. Ward regards Jesus' exhortation to his disciples in the Gospel of John to "abide in Me as I abide in you,"[11] as "axiomatic for an account for a Christian act." Jesus' exhortation in the Gospel of John leaves no room within Christian subjectivity for the self-sufficiency of the Cartesian subject which the Council documents seem to presume. Instead, the subjectivity that seems to be implicated in any Christian action would be one that is profoundly relational. Christian subjectivity is always set within the horizons of placing one's self in another, namely Christ. This immediately sets the tone for all subjectivities in which each one only *is* within another. Conversely, the Christian subject is never fully autonomous because there is an abiding *of* Christ within the self, and this in turn forms the blueprint of Christian subjectivity in which all Christian subjects, as they are placed *within* others, also *have* others placed within themselves.[12]

The operation of this form of relationality in subjectivity is manifest in one of the most basic elements of subjectivity, namely at the level of knowledge. For Ward all knowledge, including knowledge of self, is far from a commodity to be held but is constituted in a profoundly relational process. Knowledge is drawn not only from oneself but also from others, because knowledge involves not only cognition but very concrete acts of corporeal practice, and these practices are always taking place "within the context of other performances."[13] The reference to the "context of other performances" is highly significant on a number of levels and shall be explored in later sections. For now it is important to understand that Ward is providing an insightful critique of the

10. Ward, "Christian Act," 36, 42.
11. John 15:4
12. Ward, *Politics of Discipleship*, 187.
13. Ward, *Christ and Culture*, 95.

notion of subjectivity implicitly acknowledged by the Council as part of the Christian heritage. The Christian agent is, contrary to the Cartesian subject, always in process and always affected and formed by its surroundings. Ward's critique is potent because it shows knowledge to be never "stored" but always "transferred" in a series of corporeal exchanges, such that "knowing ... is continually caught up in communicating and in the communications of others."[14] Knowledge of self is also thus always caught up within a network of relational exchange.

The Neutrality and Telos of an Act

Apart from the Conciliar presumption of the Cartesian agent over and against a more Augustinian subjectivity, two other presumptions allowed for the Council's acceptance of Maritain's split between the temporal and the divine spheres. The first is the neutrality of the institutional forms of any act, which assumes that all acts are ideationally empty and can only be given substance by the intentions of the strong Cartesian subject. The second is the ability for the act to have its own *telos* in isolation of the other practices that occur around it. As Ward indicated above, accepting a Foucauldian conception of the discursive rather than the static subject of the Enlightenment would lead one to favor a more Augustinian conception of the person who is not entirely sure of himself and thus is always in the process of change and transformation. This decentring of the Cartesian subject thus undermines one of the central presumptions the Council adopted in its engagement with the modern world generally, and its treatment of the social justice of ecumenism specifically. If one were to accept Ward's critiques of this central notion of agency outlined above, it would also mean that it would be difficult to defend these two latter presumptions about neutrality and *telos*.

Understanding how the notion of an act being neutral can be a problematic one requires a return to the conception of

---

14. Ibid., 95–96.

knowledge as more than merely cognitive categories. If one accepts that knowledge does not just emit from mere cognitive reflection but also from practice, then one should also concur with critical theorists, such as Louis Althusser and Ernst Bloch, that there exists an intimate "theory-practice relationship." While theories are what instruct, infuse meaning into and ultimately bear the possibilities for transforming practices,[15] only the existence of a distinct practice can explicate the implications and possibilities of theory.[16] Furthermore, the credibility of ideas and their dynamic potential could only be realised by their being concretised in some kind of praxis.[17] If that is true, then the actual form a practice takes cannot be considered to be ideationally neutral. Rather, the specific form of a practice can only come as a result of the acceptance of certain foundational ideas, even if that assent were not articulated or even recognized. This point has been taken up by a number of sociologists, who speak of practices forming affective forestructures that in turn act on the person engaging in that practice without that person's foreknowledge. Peter Berger and Thomas Luckmann, for instance, have argued that practices considered to be in keeping with objective reality are often foregrounded by a series of "plausibility structures." These are often unarticulated pre-theoretical principles that are legitimated through a series of repetitive performance and "suppl[y] the institutionally appropriate rules of conduct" and "designate all situations falling within them."[18] In a similar vein, Pierre Bourdieu spoke of persons gravitating towards particular beliefs or practices because of the pull of a *habitus* or "community of dispositions"[19] which "acts within [agents] . . . as the organizing principle of their actions,"[20] and in turn makes one predisposed to gravitate towards seeing things in a particular way

---

15. Smith, *Introducing Radical Orthodoxy*, 166.

16. Althusser, *For Marx*, 172; Bloch, *Principle of Hope*, 268; Milbank, *Theology and Social Theory*, 380.

17. Davis, *Theology and Political Society*, 17.

18. Berger and Luckmann, *Social Construction of Reality*, 64–65.

19. Bourdieu, *Outline of a Theory of Practice*, 35.

20. Ibid., 18.

Justice, Unity, and the Hidden Christ

and regarding that as a "possible" or "credible" way of seeing reality. However, this *habitus* is not a naturally occurring category, but the result of being immersed in a pre-cognitive "field," which is a "social universe"[21] or "structure of social positions socially marked by the social properties of [the social universe's] occupants, through which they manifest themselves."[22] This means that the institutional shape of a particular practice, and even a person's positioning within social space, will convey a particular regime of knowledge to the agent, often before the agent is aware of it. What is more, each practice also ultimately points to a proclamation of an ultimate allegiance to a particular polity.[23] Precisely because of the form and language of the practices engaged, the ideas that are attached to that practice can become resistant to the change that the intentions of the agent seek to bring. Rather, the meaning of the cognitive categories of the agent can become modified and even transformed when it is engaged with and adapted to the particular institutional forms of practices, rituals and even geographical layouts, all of which carry a particular tradition with their own rationalities that act on the agent.[24]

Thus, far from the agent making the act an extension of his will, it is more likely that his participation in an act will incorporate the practitioner into a particular regime of knowledge or social imaginary. The other major implication is that the body rather than the mind will become the new site of power precisely because it has become the new "base for communicative activity."[25] The communicative power of the body is due to the fact that it has

---

21. Bourdieu, *Field of Cultural Production*, 162.
22. Ibid., 71.
23. Ward, *Politics of Discipleship*, 191.
24. MacIntyre, *Whose Justice? Which Rationality?* See esp. ibid., 355. For an interesting look into the link between ideas, affective dispositions and urban design, see Gorringe, *Theology of the Built Environment*. See in particular ibid., ix, where Gorringe argues that "wittingly or unwittingly every design for council estates, every barrio, every skyscraper, every out of town supermarket, expresses a view of the human, embodies an ethic."
25. Gil, *Metamorphoses of the Body*, 107.

become the very site on which a particular imaginary inscribes itself and challenges others.[26]

This conception of the body has a profound impact on agency for the agent who, by engaging in a particular practice, is thus more likely to become an imaginary's transmitter rather than its progenitor. What is more, the body is not left intact by its involvement in that imaginary. Foucault provides the most graphic account for the body in this process of recruitment, whereby the body is "mark[ed] . . . train[ed and] . . . tortur[ed]" into an instrument that "emits signs."[27] But more than that, such rigorous reformation of the body does not just turn it into an emitter of signs that still enjoy some distance from the authorities whose interest lies in their emission. According to Foucault's account of the Panopticon, "reinforcing the . . . gaze" of the guard occurs because those being guarded become so subject to the architectures of power that they themselves become their own guards.[28] The formation of knowledge categories is synonymous with making the subject's body coextensive with that imaginary.[29] In the same way that responding to the Gospel involves "putting on Christ"[30] and mimicking Christ to the point of becoming *alter-Christos*,[31] acceptance of the imaginary's knowledge is to accept not just mere recruitment into the practices of the imaginary, but also of a corporeal transformation into the very image of the imaginary into which the subject will be immersed. Subject and imaginary will, just as Christ hoped for with respect to his disciples and God, "all be one."[32] All individuals inevitably become, "walking and talking

---

26. Baudrillard, *Symbolic Exchange and Death*, 101–21. A similar and more theologically focussed take on the incorporation of the body into communicating regimes of knowledge can be found in Cavanaugh, *Torture and Eucharist*, 48–70.

27. Foucault, *Discipline and Punish*, 25.

28. Bell, *Liberation Theology*, 26.

29. Smith, *Who's Afraid of Postmodernism?*, 92.

30. Rom 13:14.

31. Smith, *Who's Afraid of Postmodernism?*, 106.

32. John 17:22.

fragments of a given society... embody[ing]... the essential core of the institutions and significations of their society."[33]

This is relevant for the purposes of the present analysis of paragraph 12 of *Unitatis Redintegratio* because the concept of engaging in practices in a Christian manner requires more than the mere "infusion of Christian principles" through the intentions of the practitioner. Just what constitutes this "more" will be explored in later sections, but for now it must be observed that engaging in a particular form of practice implicates the practitioner into a particular regime of knowledge that may be resistant to the practitioner's intentions and may even modify the contours of the practitioner's intentions.

Treating the presumption concerning the neutrality of an act's institutional form would put one in a better position to deal with the second concerning the *telos* of any act. Recall that this book had asserted earlier that the Council Fathers adopted a presumption of the strong Cartesian subject. The adoption of this kind of subjectivity impacts on the presumptions one would have on the inner reality of that subject's actions. In the first place, the strength of the Cartesian subject would lead one to believe that realities have no other cause than the exercise of the individual's will. Because the individual's will is what creates reality, each act can become a reality unto itself, since the will can hermetically seal the reality of that one action from those of others.[34] While it may be true that the institutional shape of practices carry within them a certain language and particular ideational content that resists modification through intentions, it does not mean that such content is hermetically sealed off within that practice alone. This is because, as Ward mentioned above, one performance is never isolated but always set "within the context of other performances."

33. Castoriadis, "Radical Imagination and the Social Instituting Imaginary," 332.

34. The philosophical link between the strength of the Cartesian subject and the reality within human action can be traced back to the thought of Duns Scotus and William of Ockham, both of whom created the space for the growth of the radical autonomy of the will. For an elaboration of their thought and their effects, see Pinckaers, *Sources of Christian Ethics*, 242.

In the same way that the meaning of words can only be discerned by the sentence that forms its context, the *telos* of an act "cannot be determined without an appreciation of the practices that situate the act," that is, without reference to the practices that form its context.[35] Ward gives the example of the giving of loose change to a beggar as an action that is in and of itself ambiguous in its meaning. While that act can be seen as an act of charity, it can also be seen as "an act of condescension, an act of obedience [to another], a way to alleviate guilt, a way to make a political statement . . . an so forth." Just which one it constitutes is determined by "the social and economic circumstances circumscribing both agent and action, and the social and/or religious mores that encourage or discourage such an action."[36] The imaginary creates forestructures that act as "the horizon of meaning through which understanding becomes possible."[37] Because of this it can be said that the meaning of the one act is always articulated through the imaginary in which that particular act is embedded.

Set against this backdrop, the assumptions adopted by the Council Fathers that acts of social justice in and of themselves can so transparently proclaim Christ to all will start to appear problematic. The clarity of Christ's servant-hood as the cultural language of an act of social justice could only be discerned if the practices that make up its context carry within them a similar Christic logic. But here one must note that in our contemporary context, the act of social justice is virtually always circumscribed by the dominance of the nation state as the high watermark of sociality. This might sound like a continuation of one of the main threads of Jacques Maritain's ecclesiology, until one realises that the horizons of the modern nation state are in postmodernity framed within the hegemony of consumer capitalism. This raises the question: if context determines the overall *telos* of any particular act, and if an act of social justice is melting into a market oriented cultural form, would that act provide the grounds for a proclamation of Christ which both evangelises

---

35. Ward, *Politics of Discipleship*, 191.
36. Ibid.
37. Veling, *Living in the Margins*, 31.

and unifies Christian communities? In other words, is an act of social justice in a market context a Christian act?

The Presumption of the Free Church in Civil Society

Some may object to the deterministic nature of context, arguing that there exist spaces where agents like the Church would be free to pursue their public activities without being coerced by other agents within that space. More specifically, they would argue instead that the Church operating in a neutral civic space can unproblematically proclaim Christ through their actions of social justice without its logic being interfered with by its social context. Such objections are referring to the notion of ideologically free public sphere or civil society, a "free space between private lives and large scale institutions . . . with a relatively open and participatory character."[38] Agents in this "free space" can thus simultaneously break out of the isolation of the private sphere, be free from the coercive force and cultural logic of both state and market, and also respect a separation of Church and state by its avoiding direct interface with the exercise of sovereign power.[39] At the same time, through the engagement of "patterns of work that have public dimensions," agents would be able to reclaim and redefine the nature of the public they are in, thereby breaking through the isolation of civil society and eventually transforming the *polis*.[40] The notion of a free Church in a neutral civil society was a presumption that was adopted in its nascent form during the Council and is especially salient in the minds of those that seek to give the Church a more public and ecumenical witness in the post-Conciliar period. It is argued that an analysis in a discursive key would reveal that such presumptions overestimate the level of freedom of the agent in civil society, and that civil society eventually will give way to the

---

38. Evans and Boyte, *Free Spaces*, 17–18.

39. Heywood, *Political Theory*, 56–57.

40. Boyte and Kari, *Building America*, 202. See also Walzer, "Civil Society Argument," 115.

logic of the market and once again make the Church an extension of its market context.

One should turn to John Courtney Murray in order to understand the mind of the Church with respect to the relationship between Church, society and state. Murray had established himself as an international authority on the Church's public witness in a modern context long before the Second Vatican Council. Murray argued that in constitutional governance, a constitutional framework limited the size of the state and that allowed for the flourishing of a distinct and common sphere of activity in which all could participate freely precisely because such spheres are beyond the reach of proper state coercive intervention.[41] The notion of limiting governments and creating distinct and free social spheres beyond the grasp of sovereign control was a compelling combination for the Council Fathers. So compelling, in fact, that Murray was invited to act as a consultant and drafter of one key Conciliar document that engaged with this specific issue, the declaration of religious freedom *Dignitatis Humanae*.[42] From the beginning, the document sought to ensure the individual's freedom of thought and the "demand for freedom in human society," by "placing constitutional limits . . . to the powers of government, in order that there may be no encroachment on the rightful freedom of the person and of associations."[43] A statement like this constitutes not only a direct articulation of civil society, but also an indirect adoption of it as the proper zone of activity for the Church. In light of this recognition of civil society as a free sphere for the Church's public witness, the Council Fathers seem to similarly keep this same neutral sphere at the forefront of their consideration of different churches making a common proclamation of Christ through a common act of social justice. In other words, when the Council Fathers ratified the final draft of *Unitatis Redintegratio*, one could argue that such acts of social justice were

41. J. C. Murray, "Civil Unity and Religious Integrity," 45–78; J. C. Murray, "Problem of Religious Freedom," 127–98.

42. The full text of this document can be found in Flannery, *Vatican Council II*, 551–68.

43. *Dignitatis Humanae*, 1.

able to proclaim Christ because they took place in the ideologically free neutral sphere of civil society.

To understand the problems with this position, one must first understand that the relationship between civil society and the state is not one of complete independence. In spite of their anti-statist tendencies, advocates of civil society still regard the state form as the most mature form of human organisation. This stateward orientation of civil society is framed in normative terms by Michael Walzer who, even in arguing for the importance of civil society in developing solidarity, spoke of the need for the state to "compel association members to think about a common good, beyond their own conceptions of the good life."[44] This is why, according to James Scott, all civil society actors are ultimately encouraged to "see like a state."[45] Despite its conceptual independence from the state, the effectiveness of civil society in theory comes precisely from its supposed capacity to influence the levers of state. The notion of civil society as a zone free from the reach of the state is qualified by a thread of power whose logical flow is almost always headed towards state institutions.

The second thing to note is that the existence of civil society, or more specifically the keeping of the civility of civil society, is almost always dependent on the state. Richard John Neuhaus remarked that civil society necessarily implicates a plurality of actors "government, corporations, education, communications, religion," all of which "challenge, check and compete with one another."[46] This is echoed in many ways by George Weigel, who argued that the Church, as a member of civil society, must translate "religiously based moral claims and arguments into concepts that can be heard and contested by fellow citizens of different faiths."[47] Although Aristotle affirmed the importance of different types of citizens living in the same *polis*, he still presumed the necessity of a shared *telos*. This is to be contrasted with the remarks of Neuhaus

44. Walzer, "Civil Society Argument," 129.
45. Scott, *Seeing Like a State*.
46. Neuhaus, *Naked Public Square*, 84.
47. Weigel, *Catholicism*, 116.

and Weigel. They rightly affirm the myriad of different types of actors, but combining that affirmation with the use of the words "challenge," "compete" and "contested" suggests an added presumption that there is within civil society itself a lack of a common end. Where such shared ends are lacking the state, being the sole legitimate bearer of coercive power, inevitably steps in as either the main arbiter over civil society or the most dominant agent within it. This plays itself out in the state either becoming an expression of a Rousseauan "general will" or as the referee between conflicting parties. The state is also the most dominant agent within civil society for another reason: it remains the largest single employer, whether directly as an employer of public servants or indirectly as the focal point of tenders by private commercial players. The reasons of state therefore permeate through the borders of the supposedly independent civil society. When the logic of state becomes so pervasive, what often happens is that "the supposedly free debate of the public square [or civil society] is disproportionately affected by the state."[48]

A third thing to note is the collapse of state and society into the market. Michael Hardt,[49] Kenneth Surin,[50] and Antonio Negri[51] have observed that, rather than democracy liberating society from the logic of markets, markets have conspired with state via democracy to absorb society and form a single cultural nexus. State power in a post-Cold War context has evolved and "extend[ed] throughout social space in the channels created by the institutions of civil society."[52] In addition, both the reasons of state and civil society in liberal modes of government have become "particularly attuned to the precepts of political economy."[53] Thus, rather than becoming that celebrated zone of freedom against state and market, civil society had actually become the primary zone

48. Cavanaugh, *Theopolitical Imagination*, 71.
49. Hardt, "Withering of Civil Society," 27–44.
50. Surin, "Marxism(s)," 42–46.
51. Negri, *Politics of Subversion*.
52. Hardt, "Withering of Civil Society," 33.
53. Bell, *Liberation Theology*, 29.

through which the state extended the "autonomous functioning of economic processes within society."[54] This is significant because the Council Fathers had presumed the liberty of civil society just as civil society was being domesticated by state and market. Now, one has arrived at a situation in which economic, political and social imperatives have merged. Culture now "obeys the logic of the market and the political apparatuses in turn create spaces for capital to operate." Under such circumstances "what is permissible as a public discourse increasingly obeys the logic of accumulation."[55] All actions thus have their ends directed towards the processes of capitalist production and consumption.

Conclusion: The Church as Chaplain to the Capitalist Order

This foisting of an assessment of an essentially third-millenium postmodern social condition onto a document that was drafted forty years before may be a bit unfair. However, for now one can draw on no other comprehensive statement that is indicative of the mind of the church on the issue of linking ecumenism and social justice. What is more easily discernible, however, is the relationship between the Church and capitalism. This is indicated not so much within the text of *Unitatis Redintegratio* itself, for that document did not seem to indicate any inconsistency between faith and any particular form of economics. However, if one appreciates the totality of the other Conciliar documents, one would notice that none seem to indicate any essentially confessionally based opposition to the state or market form as such. This is largely due to the broader Conciliar enthusiasm for the autonomy of the laws within the secular sphere from ecclesiastical interference, which meant that economics as a science in the secular sphere was immune from any theological critique. This line of thinking concerning economics was more explicitly articulated by Paul VI, who steered the

---

54. Burchell, "Peculiar Interests," 139.
55. Cavanaugh, *Theopolitical Imagination*, 71.

course for the Council in its latter stages. In *Ecclesiam Suam*, the pope spoke of the necessity to bring a spirit of poverty to a world that was obsessed by material wealth.[56] Nevertheless, he said that such a spirit presented "no obstacle to the proper understanding and rightful application of the important laws of economics . . . a subject which has made great strides within recent years . . . [and] has been responsible for the progress of civilization."[57] The spirit of poverty could inform the Church on economic matters, but that did not let the Church interfere with the unshakable laws of economics itself. In this statement, Paul inadvertently articulated the mind of the Council Fathers concerning the Church's relation to capitalism.

As part of the secular sphere, capitalism was implicitly deemed an economic science that imposed limits on the scope of the Church's social critique, since capitalism had become regarded as an autonomous cultural form in the eyes of the Council. The Church as a specialist within its own spiritual sphere acted as an acultural deposit of values and would find its institutional place in the world not by dominating over other secular institutional forms. When the autonomy of the temporal sphere was recognized as an ecclesial principle, the church unavoidably presumed the supremacy of secular authorities in what were deemed to be secular matters. Therefore, the Church can only conceive of its institutional life in terms of being a subsection of a larger, secular social reality which has rightfully achieved its own dominance in the temporal sphere. All manner of the Church's embodiment, whether through its institutions, works, or modes of thinking, have to conform to the hegemony of secular regimes of management. Under such circumstances, the Church effectively becomes what Michael Budde calls the chaplain to the dominant secular imaginary. Its relevance is determined in so far as it proves itself to be useful to the sustaining of the status quo. The Church's attitude must, in the words of John Howard Yoder, be "'positive' toward the rulers of the particular unity of society which [s]he serves, towards its aims

---

56. *ES*, 54.
57. Ibid., 55.

and towards its preservation." If the Church were to undertake any critique that simultaneously respects the "autonomy of culture," it must first "be filtered through [her] fundamental acceptance of the system at it is."[58] The Church as servant of the world, when its embodiment is conceived as but a subsection of a larger temporal reality, will effectively *co-opt* the cultural logic of the status quo.

In so doing, the church eventually becomes *co-opted* into sustaining, sanctifying and ultimately extending the capitalist order.[59] When the Church's critique has become absorbed into the status quo via the respect for the autonomy of culture, it will eventually place itself within what Kieran Flanagan calls "the nexus of culture in the marketplace" and such critiques will have the Church end up having to "endorse everything, all commodities, idols and artefacts, indiscriminately."[60] The Church's role inevitably becomes one of "helping society with questions of shared 'values' and 'meaning'" (with "society" here being defined by patterns of consumption),[61] or being a guide to "empower individuals to find the proper balance as the individual negotiates his or her way within the consumerist cycle" while leaving that cycle intact.[62] If the church is spatially but a subsection of a capitalist dominated order, then would having capitalism as the dominant imaginary be amenable to a Christian's ascribing a Christian *telos* to any act that is clear to all, so that the Gospel may be proclaimed to all and visible unity be achieved between Christians? Answering this question would be the focus of the next chapter.

---

58. Yoder, *For the Nations*, 119.

59. Budde, *(Magic) Kingdom of God*, 120. See also Budde and Brimlow, *Christianity Incorporated*, 140.

60. Flanagan, *Enchantment of Sociology*, 15.

61. Budde, *(Magic) Kingdom of God*, 120.

62. Wright, *Telling God's Story*, 133–34.

CHAPTER 3

Liberalism, Capitalism, Church and Ecumenism

Nexus or Battlelines?

Introduction

The previous chapter outlined the unarticulated presumptions adopted by the Council Fathers concerning the Cartesian subject, the neutrality of an act's form, the ability for any single act to have its own *telos*, and the neutrality of civil society. It then evaluated these presumptions in light of Foucault's discursive turn as it has been developed by Graham Ward. It argued that, contrary to the presumption of the static Cartesian subject that can decisively impose its will on any object, an agent is always "in process" and being formed by his social context. Contrary to the presumption of the neutrality of the form of an act, this book argued that each practical form is always intimately tied to a particular theoretical base. It also argued that, contrary to the presumption of the agent being able to ascribe a *telos* to just a single act, an act is often going to have its ends defined by the logic of other practices that make up its context. Finally, in response to assertions of the neutrality of civil society, this book argued that the modern notion of freedom within civil society is illusory and subject to the control of the logic

Justice, Unity, and the Hidden Christ

of state and market. It was argued in the previous chapter that the adoption of these presumptions created a spatial problematic for the Church. By adopting these presumptions, the Council posited the Church as but a subsection of an autonomous secular cultural reality. Furthermore, in adopting these modern presumptions, the Council Fathers had posited the Church as a chaplain to the secular status quo, one whose horizons were circumscribed by the state and the market. Ultimately, the adoption of these presumptions entrenched not only capitalism, but also the liberalism that underpinned it, since it is impossible for anyone to advocate the primacy of capitalism as a cultural form, without extending also its liberal underpinnings.[1] The question arises: would liberalism's circumscribing the Church's practice of social justice make it more or less amenable to proclaim Christ in an ecumenical manner, as was envisioned in paragraph 12 of *Unitatis Redintegratio*?

This chapter will argue that the concession given to liberalism by the Council undermined engendering visible Christian unity through social justice. The Conciliar capitulation to liberalism undermines the explicitly Christian content within any act of social justice and replaces it with a market oriented cultural logic with anti-Christian underpinnings. The anti-Christian nature of the market's cultural logic stems from the modern imperative to fragment and atomise, thus undermining any communal foundations towards visible Christian unity and replacing fundamental communion with fundamental conflict. Thus, the critique of the Conciliar capitulation to capitalism and liberalism is at once political and theological. To begin understanding the theological and social aspects of this critique, one needs to analyze the differences in anthropologies that are presumed by Christianity on the one hand and capitalism on the other, as well as the differences in the cultural trajectories that emerge from these anthropologies.

---

1. Budde and Brimlow, *Christianity Incorporated*, 132.

Trinity and Idiocy

It is almost cliché to note that Christian anthropology centers around the theme of man being made in the *imago dei*. In recent times, the definition of what that imaging means has undergone a dramatic shift, with highly significant cultural implications. Instead of the traditional tendency to draw an analogy between human and divine rationality, the weight of contemporary Christian anthropology has shifted its emphasis to the theme of the constitution of a single Godhead by three persons.[2] Instead of looking at God's being as constituted by a unity of reason, the Trinitarian focus sought to recover a patristic understanding of God who is recognizable only insofar as He is marked by three persons engaged in relations of self-giving love.[3] It would thus be "unthinkable to speak about the 'one God' without speaking of . . . communion."[4] Thus, if human persons are made in the image of God, from the standpoint of Trinitarian theology, a person is no longer looked at as a discrete category. Instead, its definition is set in relation to other categories. That is, the person is fundamentally constituted by his or her relationships to others and to God.[5] The explorations of Foucault's discursive subject, the acquisition of knowledge in general and knowledge of the self in particular as trans-personal categories powerfully demonstrate this need for relation when defining the contours of the individual. The disperse sources of the self would make it difficult to identify something in the world that is not of the individual self. The person, according to the discursive turn and Trinitarian anthropology, is thus de-centered in that being does not come from the individual self, nor do social processes end in the individual.[6] Indeed, the retrieval of the medieval notion of the Trinity as an anthropological category would mean that

---

2. Grenz, *Social God*, 5.
3. Zizioulas, *Being as Communion*, 16.
4. Ibid., 17.
5. Cunningham, "Trinity," 189.
6. M. C. Taylor, *Erring*, 139.

relation is just as important as the persons within that relation, since the latter can only be defined via the former.

The Trinitarian notion of self defined by relation with others must be contrasted against the anthropological presumptions of both liberalism and capitalism, which begin from a position of idiocy. In its original Greek meaning, *idios* refers to a position of selfish isolation from the community. Liberalism is idiotic in the sense that it presumes the person to be fundamentally an individual prior to and independent of any communal belonging. The individual is autonomous and self-contained, and thus enters into communal association through no greater force than that of the individual will, hence the modern demarcation of a variety of organisations, social clubs, churches, political, educational and business organisations, as "voluntary associations." Furthermore, the will's decision to enter into communion emerges from giving primacy to a rational calculation that aim to maximise the individual's advantage.[7] The rational, autonomous individual is posited as the primary sociopolitical unit and takes precedence over any kind of communal association. Liberal political theory thus posits associations to be either facilitators of the extension of the individual will, or at worst, a threat to the individual's autonomy through any form of corporate discipline. The anthropological primacy given to the individual over the community, as well as the imperative to ensure freedom—defined as the removal of constraints on the exercise of the individual will—manifest themselves in two mutually reinforcing modes in the secular sphere. First, human rights discourse as the protection of the dignity of the human person as fundamentally an individual becomes the normative platform by which much of secular politics proceeds.[8] Also, as Milton Friedman would argue, capitalism eventually becomes the network of economic practices that eventually buttress the idea of freedom as liberty from the threat posed by others.[9] While the coupling of

---

7. Cavanaugh, *Theopolitical Imagination*, 44.

8. Falk, *Human Rights Horizons*. See also Ignatieff, "Human Rights as Politics," 3–52.

9. Friedman, *Capitalism and Freedom*, 7–17.

human rights discourse with capitalism may seem counter-intuitive, it is interesting to note that the progenitors of the modern discourse of rights were the same progenitors of bourgeois capitalism. Far from being juxtaposed against each other, the liberal view of individual rights actually coalesced with the notion of the maximisation of individual wealth.[10] The relevance of this line of thought would be demonstrated below, but for now, one should note that Christian action begins from an anthropology that is severely at odds with action framed by liberalism.

Harmony and Violence

The inconsistencies between the anthropologies assumed by Christianity on the one hand, and liberalism and capitalism on the other, become less abstract (and indeed more problematic for the Christian) as these anthropologies work themselves out in competing modes of human relations. Christian anthropology in a Trinitarian key proceeds from the creative, self-giving relations of Father, Son, and Spirit as the primary reality from which all other realities hang. These are relations that are fundamentally harmonious. Furthermore, this transcendent Trinity is not superimposing harmony on an otherwise chaotic, pre-existing category called "the world." Rather, there was in the beginning nothing, and it is out of this "formless void" that the Trinity in relation, via acts of self-donation, created the world and the order within it. Order, harmony and abundance were part of the original condition within creation. Therefore Trinitarian anthropology, as part of this creation, must similarly be grounded in an ontology that reflects its Creator, namely one of original harmony.[11] Because harmony is the fundamental social condition, and because self-giving relations

---

10. Shapiro, *Evolution of Rights in Liberal Theory*, 302–3. The notion of capitalism's compatibility with the promotion of individual rights can be seen in neoliberal works such as Friedman who was cited earlier, as well as some of the more critical literature. See for instance Arblaster, *Rise and Decline of Western Liberalism*, 55–91.

11. Cunningham, "Trinity," 196.

are foundational to giving meaning to any notion of personhood, there cannot be a closing off of one from the other. Instead, there is the imperative of being constantly open to relations with others, in an economy marked by the constant giving of oneself to another. This self-donation is possible because creation in its original form is seen as the outpouring of God's overwhelming abundance into history.[12] This is so even when creation became fallen, for that divine abundance became manifest and consummated within creation through the unsolicited self-giving of Christ on the cross. Creation is aneconomic in a sense because it is marked with a fundamental plenitude that is without scarcity.[13] Therefore, it would be unnecessary to entertain any desire for competition over resources which is fundamental to capitalism. Indeed, assuming the desire for such competition to be built into creation can only proceed from a post-lapsarian indulging of sin and division as the fundamental condition of creation.[14]

On the other hand, if one apprehends the secular sphere as consisting of the liberal autonomous individual that precedes all communion, and if one assumes that rationality for such individuals consists of the preservation and/or maximization of individual benefit, the kinds of communion one enters into is always going to be marked by risk, since there is the suspicion that in such communions, liberalism's fundamental category—individual autonomy—comes under threat as each individual takes advantage of another. Relations in such circumstances emit from an originary chaos and violence becomes the foundational characteristic of all social relations. This is the so called "state of nature" envisioned by Thomas Hobbes and assumed implicitly by many liberal theorists from John Locke onwards. The main tasks of communal

12. Ibid., 197.

13. Bell, "Only Jesus Saves," 211–12.

14. Such an assumption has pervaded even elements in political theology, within which Carl Schmitt stands as a prime example. In chapters 3 and 4 of his *Concept of the Political*, Schmitt spoke of a division between friends and enemies as an inescapable and fundamental sociopolitical reality, so much so that to exclude this division is to negate politics altogether. See Schmitt, *Concept of the Political*.

relations between autonomous self-maximizing individuals then are the furthering the purposes of the individual and the management of violence that is to be exerted by other autonomous self-maximizing individuals. According to William Cavanaugh, when the social fabric is marked by and ends with violence by self-seeking individuals, such relations are almost inevitably going to be contractual in nature, since they not only manage the supposedly original violence within such relations, but also guarantee the stability of such relations by the use of force.[15] Ultimately, the liberal autonomous individual is dependent on his membership in the social contract with the state, because the state is seen to be the most proficient wielder of force and thus the most efficient protector of the individual. Social relations in a liberal mode then take a sinister turn, for if this reading is correct, the protection of the state will become synonymous with the protection of individual liberty. The defence of liberty then would become the justification to the resort to all means necessary to protect the state, even to the point of using violence against that state's own citizens.[16] Violence then, does not become the anomaly that the state fixes, but is built into the maintenance of the state and the relations within it. When framed by liberalism, any act of social justice eventually can become complicit with maintaining a social fabric which is atomizing and fundamentally grounded in conflict and coercion.

The relations of violence in liberalism continues, and assumes its most sinister form, in relations framed by capitalism. Capitalism actualizes liberal modes of relations because, at one level, capitalism operates on the basis of the maximization of accumulation of material goods for individual benefit. At another level it intensifies liberal individualism because capitalism functions on a foundation of exchange of alienable objects from individuals in contractual relationships. In such relations, the barriers between giver, gift, and recipient as autonomous hermetically sealed categories are maintained. The exchangeability of goods and services works on the idea that what is exchanged can be shorn off from the community

---

15. Cavanaugh, *Theopolitical Imagination*, 45.
16. Žižek, "'Thrilling Romance of Orthodoxy,'" 54.

from which it comes and the persons that participate in it.[17] Indeed, capitalism insures exchangeability of all commodities by dissolving the notion of community altogether, dissolving the communal networks of the village, family and church, and entrenching in their stead a series of hub-and-spokes-type relations between individuals mediated by contracts.[18] Through capitalism, then, the continuation of the primacy of the liberal individual is ensured.

If capitalism continues the liberal protection of individual, it would also extend the relations of fundamental violence presumed by liberalism. According to Dan Bell, capitalism's triumph lies in its capture and discipline of desire to the logic of the market. As alluded to earlier, unlike the Trinitarian presumption of plenitude, the market institutionalizes the post-lapsarian notion of fundamental scarcity and competition. The fulfilment of desire under conditions of scarcity must inevitably become a matter of "capture and possession—combat and sheer assertion."[19] The post-Cold War proliferation and intensification of capitalist modes of production is accompanied with an increased volatility that produces a culture of pessimism and fear.[20] Escape from fear becomes dependent on the accumulation of material goods so as to assure physical, psychological and emotional integrity. Such accumulation generates illusions of stability, but according to Cavanaugh, capitalism can only function out of a certain detachment to the goods accumulated. In other words, capitalism's drive to generate constant consumption of new goods emits out of an inbuilt volatility that itself emerges out of "detach[ing] us from material production, producers and even the products we buy."[21] Consumption then paradoxically unveils the fleeting nature of the security brought about by accumulation, which leads to either an intensifying of what is essentially nihilistic behavior or a lashing out in acts of violence and domination against other consumers

17. Cavanaugh, *Theopolitical Imagination*, 47–48.
18. Nisbet, *Quest for Community*, 104.
19. Bell, "Only Jesus Saves," 202.
20. Bell, "Politics of Fear and the Gospel of Life," 65.
21. Cavanaugh, *Being Consumed*, 36–37.

in a desperate attempt to regain control.²² Left alone, the proliferation and intensification of such relations can only degenerate into cycles of inequality, conflict and conquests.²³ Thus, if the social context of an act of social justice is so circumscribed by the logic of capitalism, the church as chaplain would be only extending the cultural logic of the market, and the violent relations that would emit from that logic.

Difference and Conformity

Because of the illusory nature of the neutrality of the modern public sphere entertained by the Council Fathers, the Conciliar concession to the secular sphere also failed them in addressing one fundamental concern of ecumenism, namely the appreciation of difference within an otherwise united Body of Christ. The Council assumed with liberal theory that the trajectory of sociopolitical development was marked by what *Gaudium et Spes* labelled a growing "plurality of cultures,"²⁴ which resulted in a legitimate diversity of philosophical, religious and political assumptions that underpinned a diversity of worldviews.²⁵ According to liberal theory, such a diversity could only be celebrated when a neutral political space was carved out in which agents from these diverse backgrounds could enter, be heard, compete and eventually come to an agreement. Whilst liberal theory posits different modes by which this form of public life is achieved, two principles underpin all these differing strands of public thought which are also entertained by the Council Fathers.

22. Pickstock, "Liturgy, Art and Politics," 169.

23. Besançon, "Relative Resources," 395; Nathan, "Four Horsemen of the Apocalypse," 188–205.

24. *GS*, 53.

25. Rawls, *Political Liberalism*, xx. *Gaudium et Spes* spoke of a diversity of "styles of life and multiple scales of values arise from the diverse manner of using things, of laboring, of expressing oneself, of practicing religion, of forming customs, of establishing laws and juridic institutions, of cultivating the sciences, the arts and beauty" (*GS*, 53). Although the terminology is different, there remain very substantial similarities.

One such binding principle is that of the toleration of difference, which has become one of the most fundamental tropes of liberal political philosophy.[26] Because of the liberal commitment to fundamental equality of individuals that takes precedence over any communion, it is necessary in social or political intercourse to refuse to "interfere with, constrain or check the behavior or beliefs of others," despite the fact that "the behavior and beliefs in question are disapproved of, or simply disliked."[27] Though not explicitly mentioned, it is striking that tolerance framed in this manner finds parallels in *Gaudium et Spes*, in which a key pastoral concern in engaging this plurality of cultures is the avoidance of "disturbing the life of communities . . . destroying the wisdom received from ancestors, or . . . placing in danger the character proper to each people."[28]

What also ties various strands of liberal theory together is this faith in the power of human rationality to resolve the tensions created by differences in worldviews and ways of life. Liberal theory posits that because everyone is endowed with natural reason, each person is able to live freely and take different directions in how their lives without the need for direction by communal authorities. Liberalism also has the tendency to link into a single complex the freedom of rational individuals, the reform and improvement of historical conditions and the insistence on the reliance on human reason.[29] While *Gaudium et Spes* does not explicitly stipulate any mode by which differences in worldviews are to be resolved, it does implicitly assert giving the primacy of rationalism in improving the condition of all cultures. This can be gleaned from the Conciliar imperative to bring about a "progress of culture," which is brought about by an array of cultural elements. These include sciences which "greatly develop critical judgement" and the "new ways of thinking" that have emerged out of the sociological fruits of such

---

26. Kymlicka, *Contemporary Political Philosophy*, 229.
27. Heywood, *Political Theory*, 265.
28. GS, 56.
29. Heywood, *Political Theory*, 21.

critical sciences, namely urbanisation and industrialisation.[30] This is immediately followed by an affirmation of the increase in the sense of "autonomy" and consciousness of individual authorship in the culture of their community, which can only by described by the Council as "of paramount importance for the spiritual and moral maturity of the human race."[31] This Conciliar celebration of the sciences and their outworking is nothing if not similar to liberalism's affirmation of the free exercise of human reason. It is interesting that this normative affirmation of the sciences and the progress brought about by their application by autonomous rational individuals is located immediately before reflection concerning how to deal with the situation of the plurality of cultures. This suggests, at least as far as the Council is concerned, an unproblematic coupling of the liberal celebration of rationalism with the resolution of tensions between different worldviews. In other words, the Council Fathers seem to have entertained the idea that the appreciation of difference can be brought about by following liberal theory's recipe of toleration of differing worldviews held by autonomous individuals and the aggrandisement of reason as the means to negotiate between these differences.

The question to be raised here is whether this concession by the Council is actually consistent with a Christian reading of difference as is read through a Trinitarian lens. To understand how the concept of the Triune God ties up with an appreciation of difference, it is necessary to return to the point made earlier concerning the Trinity being fundamentally a union of relations between persons. It is important to note at the outset that Trinitarian relations, contra that between liberal individuals, are not relations between equals. Jesus himself regards the Father as "greater than I,"[32] and it is important to note that the Spirit, though it moves in mysterious ways, does not move of its own accord. Rather the Holy Spirit is an agent of the Father sent in the name of the Son.[33] This is significant when one

30. *GS*, 54.
31. Ibid., 55.
32. John 14:20.
33. John 14:26.

considers Ward's Trinitarian reading of culture. For Ward, for such inequalities are inequalities in power, and it is precisely because of these power asymmetries that relations between the persons arise, not just between the persons of the Trinity, but also between all persons. The relations within the Trinity, as demonstrated by Christ in his life on earth, confirms hierarchy as part of the order of things.[34] However, Trinitarians argue that it would be premature to classify such hierarchies as inherently oppressive, as liberals would. The difference the hierarchy within the Trinity makes is that this hierarchy is constantly in motion. The persons within the Trinity are not autonomous, self-sufficient monads, but instead are steeped in their relations with other persons for their identity. Such identities are solidified only insofar as they are marked by participation with one another. To borrow Michel de Certeau's words, personhood in the Trinity requires one person to "be other and move towards the other."[35] Precisely due to the constant movement within the Trinity, these power disparities are constantly being displaced. Because these power asymmetries are framed by self-giving and interdependence and inter-participation, it is necessary that the power asymmetry constantly shifts and inverts between the parties to that relationship.[36] Such relations can only be described as relations of difference, since not only the differences in persons, but also the inequality between those persons, automatically rules out any notion of sameness. For Ward, the relations that can emerge between such persons are fundamentally "distribution[s] of differences."[37] The unity that

34. Ward, *Christ and Culture*, 87–88. It must be noted that David Cunningham, among other Trinitarian theologians, argues that the recovery of a trinitarian reading of human relations actually eliminates notions of hierarchy. See Cunningham, "Trinity," 190. However, as shall be demonstrated below, it is possible that these readings of the trinity actually absorb modern obsessions of equality among individuals, which is ironic in light of Cunningham's critique of the pervasiveness of individualism within theological notions of personhood.

35. Certeau, *Practice of Everyday Life*, 110.

36. Ward, *Christ and Culture*, 88. This for Ward is why Christ can, for example, becomes both the recipient of the footwashing by Mary, as well as the one that washes the feet of his disciples. The latter could not be read in isolation of the former.

37. Ibid.

thus emerges in Trinitarian relations is one where difference is an inherent presumption to be participated in and embraced, rather than a foreign exception to be tolerated and kept at bay.

Whilst the Trinity's unity is founded on difference, the individualism within liberalism presumes a unity that founded on conformity. The American poet Kathleen Norris remarked that the more autonomy one is supposed to enjoy, the more society "demands that we resist the notion that another might be different."[38] This can only make sense when one begins from the liberal position of radical equality between monadic individuals. According to liberal theorists like Will Kymlicka, the emphasis on the salience of communities in social intercourse places undue pressures to conform one's individual behavior to those of the group, as well as begin from a position of chauvinism vis-à-vis those belonging other traditions. This chauvinism can only be countered by the imperative to treat all equally qua individuals.[39] In other words, it becomes an imperative to begin the treatment of individuals from a position that ostensibly transcends all traditions. In other words, in order to treat each monad like others, it becomes imperative that the criterion by which you treat others is able to be shorn off from any tradition that either you or the person you want to establish relations which and can thus be transferable from one set of relations to another. The criterion of the good by which you treat others must, according to Kristen Johnson, "must not be presented as part of a larger doctrine but as its own freestanding view."[40] In so doing, one operating from a liberal standpoint is able to negotiate the tension between providing equal treatment to all individuals and respecting the traditions from which they adhere to. However, this liberal mode of celebrating of individuality often gives way to the imposition of a single mode of living, that of the life of the "citizen."[41] The ability to appreciate difference within liberalism

---

38. Norris, *Cloister Walk*, 41.

39. Kymlicka, *Liberalism, Community and Culture*.

40. Johnson, *Theology, Political Theory and Pluralism*, 44.

41. Hekman, *Feminism, Identity and Difference*, 13. A genealogy of the emphasis on conformity within liberalism can be seen in Wolin, *Politics and*

presupposes a kind of sameness in terms of universalisation of "metamoral values," coupled with the insistence that these values actually trump those that are forged by tradition.[42]

This holding of the tension between the individual and the group in liberalism could not be maintained, simply because every good, including the shedding of one's tradition in order to treat everyone equally, is always profoundly in need of its own communal space in order to properly operate. In other words, the notion of being able to relate to all individuals equally regardless of their tradition requires its own specific space maintained by a specific set of criteria and modes of behavior. This means that liberalism can allow for a plurality of traditions to operate, but only insofar as those who desire to live as individuals enjoying equal treatment did so within a liberal public space and conformed to a liberal conception of the good. In other words, in order for people from different communal traditions to coexist with one another, one ironically had to conform to a single—liberal—mandated mode of behavior and thought. This is the case despite protests that liberalism has no such intent to supplant a particular tradition as a comprehensive doctrine.[43] This comes out most acutely in liberalism's emphasis on "reasonableness" as the criterion for proper public intercourse in situations of where traditions coming from differing fundamental presumptions have to interact with one another. A person, in giving a public dimension to one's particular communal belonging, can only do so via appeal to reasons to which all seemingly "reasonable" people can "reasonably" regard as credible.[44] In order for public expressions of a particular tradition to be reasonable in their intercourse with one another, according to Rawls, several key conditions that are salient for this analysis must be met. First a tradition it must specify and prioritise certain rights and liberties. Furthermore, it must assure that all within that tradition have the means to enjoy those rights and liber-

---

Vision, 307–14.

42. Horrell, *Solidarity and Difference*, 243; Bridges, *Culture of Citizenship*, 80.

43. Rawls, *Political Liberalism*, xviii.

44. Ibid., li–lii.

ties as free and equal individuals.[45] What is more intriguing is Rawls' insistence that the articulation of the contours of those rights and freedoms must be expressed within the horizons of a deliberately cultivated public political culture. Such a public political culture must be part of a democratic society, and must set the contours of the rights and freedoms that such reasonable expressions of a tradition should articulate.[46] This political culture could only be cultivated by a process of inculcation in a series of institutions, so much so that every citizen, regardless of tradition, would nonetheless be trained to be loyal to both those institutions, and the reasonable mode of intercourse that they were meant to facilitate.[47] The postulates of liberalism, which are supposed to facilitate the maximum freedom of individuals, must necessarily be complemented by a value positive framework with concrete sites of training all peoples in a particular tradition. The ability of anyone to harmonise their particular tradition with that of liberalism becomes dependent on the ability of the former to conform to the latter.[48]

In its attempt to try and transcend the divisive nature of adherence to tradition and create a tradition-less space in which all may participate, liberalism's space had itself become a tradition which divided peoples from their own communal setting. Even more sinister is the fact that a liberal sphere of conformity is a totalizing one, one that is "impos[ed] politically, legally, socially, and culturally wherever [liberalism] has the power to do so."[49] This is pertinent to the vision of unity between different Christian communions because liberalism's imperative to ensure conformity to liberal modes of behavior mean that its tolerance of the public expressions of rival modes of communal behavior is actually severely

---

45. Ibid., xlviii, 6.

46. Ibid., 11–15. Rawls gives further elaboration of the mode of collaboration in such a democratic social setting in an essay on public reason. See Rawls, "Idea of Public Reason Revisited," 129–80. See esp. ibid., 133.

47. Johnson, *Theology, Political Theory and Pluralism*, 45.

48. Rawls, *Political Liberalism*, 163–64.

49. MacIntyre, *Whose Justice?*, 336.

restricted.[50] This represents a setback for relations between ecclesial communions because it presupposes the need for differing communions to substantially conform to a liberal alternative.[51] What this also means is that liberalism's project of negotiating the tension between individualism and communal belonging will always weigh the balance in favor of individualism, and also not allow for any individual to be even partially defined by his or her communal belongings. The Christian can thus only operate publicly is one that is shorn off of any ecclesial attachments, not only in terms of particular bodily practices, but also of cognitive categories. Because of the compulsory shearing off of any communal attachment within liberal spaces, the only kind of Christian that can operate publically is a free and rational person that is acceptable in a liberal framework, and ultimately is one that is, as Michael Sandel puts it, "wholly without character, without moral depth."[52]

Conclusion

In looking at and extrapolating from the anthropologies presumed by Trinitarian Christianity on the one hand and liberalism and capitalism on the other, this chapter has hopefully exposed the tensions that may emerge when the Church undertakes the works of social justice on terms set by the capture by the state/society/market complex of social space. Moreover, it exposed the tensions that exist between the ecumenical vision of the Conciliar Fathers of an action between different Christian communions and the insistence that such communions be abandoned and that all differences become subsumed into a flattened liberal network of individual monads.

What should become apparent in the reflections above is that if the heart of the problem of the subjugation of ecclesial action lies in the Church's subordination of its embodiment to the

50. Ibid.
51. Owen, *Religion and the Demise of Liberal Rationalism*, 117.
52. Sandel, *Liberalism and the Limits of Justice*, 179.

institutions of liberalism and capitalism as the only properly embodied social order, then the resistance must begin by the Church taking itself seriously "as a polity in its own right . . . [and] an alternative community called by God to model a distinct way of being in the world."[53] To avoid the reduction of this notion of the Church as a public to a mere pious metaphor, the Church must begin from the production of a space that it can properly call its own. This is more than a crude political calculation, since as Charles Mathewes notes, "what [may] initially seem [to be] a contingent political question [will be] revealed to be a deep and inescapable metaphysical issue."[54] Thus, in the production of properly ecclesial spaces, the Church will also properly enact its own practices with ultimately its own knowledge claims, *teloi* and sociopolitical possibilities. This would more specifically apply to the institutional forms that the actions of social justice would take, as well as the depths of ecumenism that can be entertained. Explaining just what those possibilities are will be the task of the next chapter.

---

53. Budde and Brimlow, *Christianity Incorporated*, 155.
54. Mathewes, "Pluralism, Otherness, and the Augustinian Tradition," 86.

CHAPTER 4

Leitourgia, Diakonia, and *Oikumene*

Introduction

THE PREVIOUS CHAPTERS HAVE laid out elements of the theopolitical complex which informed the uncritical adoption of modernity into sections of the Conciliar documents. It also sought to demonstrate that any theopolitical complex renders any action, including acts of social justice, at the same time a declaration of ultimate allegiance to a political configuration. Thus when spatial dominance is ceded to the state/society/market complex, even ostensibly Christian acts can declare the ultimate social reality to be something other than the Body of Christ. The works of the Church in social justice and in ecumenism are affected when the Church accepts the secular imperative to limit its embodiment to a becoming a chaplain within the state/society/market complex. This is because the prioritization of one social configuration over another would lead to the prioritization of one anthropology over another. The Church as chaplain, subordinated to the capitalist order, would make the church extend the atomized, mercenary self of the state/society/market complex, rather than the Trinitarian self of Christianity.

If the problem the Church faces is the subordination of itself to another public, the response of the Church must include "assum[ing] its proper place in the temporal realm as . . . the

Leitourgia, Diakonia, *and* Oikumene

exemplary form of human community."[1] Providing a concrete alternative communal site prevents the alternative consciousness that the Church wants to nurture from being domesticated by the dominant cultural form. In other words, the Church must embody itself as a public in its own right. However, because the Church is profoundly embedded in the world it is meant to transform, and because the form of the action determines the *telos* and the priorities of an agent, the risk lies in the Church's considering as its own practices that would further extend, rather than challenge, the secular status quo. More specifically, the risk is that the form of the Church's actions might continue to define its political program in terms that privilege statecraft as the site of the social *par excellence,* and thereby cement the Church's role as chaplain to the state/society/market complex. As was explored in the previous chapter, this would create serious tensions between the Church's salvific work as is taking place in the act of social justice on the one hand, and the liberal vision of human flourishing as enacted by the state/society/market complex on the other. The Church's ability to discern and judge the secular status quo thus becomes dependent on its spatial positioning vis-à-vis the secular imaginary. The more the Church plays the chaplain to the capitalist order, the less it will be able to stand in judgement of it. If the Church were to stand in judgement of the reality around it, it must first renounce its place as chaplain as well as renounce her tacit service to the dominant order.[2]

Renouncing the Church's role as chaplain requires re-analyzing the Church's own practices as sources for building a properly ecclesial public, with its own knowledge claims and thus own sociopolitical possibilities, both with regards to the forms actions of social justice would take and the kinds of ecumenism that can be entertained. This section would focus on how sacramental practice could become the foundation for a properly ecclesial political action, primarily by executing the presumptions of the Trinitarian anthropology mentioned above. For the purposes of this book, the

---

1. Bell, *Liberation Theology,* 144.
2. Yoder, *Royal Priesthood,* 173.

focus will be on the Eucharist as the exemplary sacramental act in which the Church could reposition itself vis-à-vis the dominant order and provide the proper basis for an ecumenical vision as enacted by cooperative works of social justice.

Justifying the Sacramental Locus

The first task of this chapter is to show the salience of sacramental practice in defining the context for the Church's social action. An entry point for this discussion is Pope Benedict's encyclical *Deus Caritas Est*.[3] In paragraph 25, Benedict states that "the Church's deepest nature is expressed in her three-fold responsibility: of proclaiming the word of God (*kerygma-martyria*), celebrating the sacraments (*leitourgia*) and exercizing the ministry of charity (*diakonia*)." Far from being self-contained components that can be excised from the other components without affecting its own character or that of the others, Benedict asserts that these three elements "presuppose each other and are inseparable."[4] To remove any one of these elements would thus render what remains nonsensical.

Benedict's observation on the link between *leitourgia* and *diakonia* touches upon an assertion of this book regarding the intimate links between the act of social justice, its context and its *telos*. While *diakonia* and *leitourgia* each declare the Church, they do not necessarily do so independent of each other. Benedict's assertion about the inter-presuppositionary nature of the three ecclesial elements implies that considering the act of *diakonia*, such as the act of social justice, as a properly ecclesial act presupposes a properly ecclesial *leitourgia*. The use of the word *leitourgia* to define sacramental ritual is key here, for it denotes not merely the worship by individuals of God, but also a work done for the sake of a collective occupying a public space. While *diakonia* can and should declare the Church, it could only do so when it simultaneously declares an allegiance to a properly ecclesial public. This

---

3. Benedict XVI, *Deus caritas est* (hereinafter *DCE*).
4. *DCE*, 25.

declaration comes not from *diakonia* in itself, but in its seamless combination with *leitourgia*.⁵ Sacramental practice is an important link to the act of social justice because it defines a public context for the act. Because of this *leitourgia* also delineates a *telos* for the act of *diakonia*, with the content of the former being defined by the *kergyma-martyria*.

If this is true, then speaking of a Christian *kerygma* in acts shorn of any ecclesial context, as is done in much modern discourse, becomes questionable. Precisely because sacramental liturgy is "the public work par excellence of the Church," shearing the Church's social work from its worship of whilst still maintaining an element of "Christian value" runs the risk of making the act anything but particularly ecclesial or even generally Christian.⁶ This is why Stanley Hauerwas points out that what is done in ethics should be indistinguishable from what is done in liturgy.⁷ Thus, quarantining the particularly ecclesial elements of the Church, namely a context defined by *leitourgia*, in favor of *diakonia* on the assumption that it will both retain a Christian *kerygma* and still find areas of commonality with other non-Catholic or even non-Christian viewpoints, will only immerse the act of *diakonia* in another non-ecclesial public context. This would make an otherwise Christian *diakonia* part of a non-ecclesial *leitourgia*, one demarcated by the state/society/market complex. If an act were circumscribed by this complex, it would mean its *telos* would be defined by a *kerygma* proclaimed by something other than the Church.⁸ It would thus be questionable if one could find sufficient

---

5. This is why Rodney Clapp considers *leitourgia* to be "the public work par excellence of the church—something that, if omitted, would mean the church was no longer the church. Far from being a retreat from the real world, worship enables Christians to see what the real world is and equips them to live in it" (see Clapp, *Peculiar People*, 114). See also Hauerwas, *Performing the Faith*, 156.

6. Clapp, *Peculiar People*, 114.

7. Hauerwas, *Better Hope*, 158.

8. James K. A. Smith speaks of secular culture having its own liturgies, which in turn declare different forms of good news, by first declaring different forms of human flourishing. For instance, he argues that when one is ritually immersed in practices from shopping to listening to talk-back radio in

ecclesial grounding on which to declare a common witness to Christ amongst different ecclesial communions in a context which is materialistic, atomistic and competitive.

Demarcating an act of social justice as a properly ecclesial act necessitates the Church to battle against its domestication via its ceding of space to the state/society/market complex. It should be clear from the analysis above that the Body of Christ must take its worship seriously as embodying a public in its own right, an exemplary public with its own space within which Christian discipleship as an embodied technology that forms the person engaging in the act of social justice. This requires a more robust taking up of social space than what is implied by *diakonia* alone, and thus challenges the monopoly of space taken up by the state/society/market complex.

The Tactical Church

It is one thing to argue that the Church must take up space a space of its own, but one must be specific as to *how* it is to take up space, lest arguments for the Church to be a public in its own right collapse into advocacy for a revival of the Church as a state form. To engage this, one must briefly look to the distinction identified by Michel de Certeau between occupying space strategically on the one hand and doing so tactically on the other.

In *The Practice of Everyday Life*, Certeau defined the strategic way of occupying space as characterised by an imperative of a social configuration to own that space, keep it under constant surveillance and exclude other forms of social embodiment. Such a mode of action presumes a "subject with will and power," against whom every other subject that occupies space is deemed a threat to be managed, if not eliminated. This creates a drive to begin all social action with a "distinguish[ing] its 'own' place . . . of its own

---

the car, one is not engaged in a rational practise of consuming for the sake of self-fulfilment. Rather, that person is engaged in a network of formation of a person into a consumer, where consumption is seen as the highest good. See Smith, *Desiring the Kingdom*. See esp. ibid., 75–88.

Leitourgia, Diakonia, *and* Oikumene

power and will." Space thus functions as a "base from which relations with an exteriority of composed of targets or threats . . . can be managed." This is usually achieved by maximizing the scope of supervision over that space, and slowly manipulating that space and coercively facilitating its transformation from a zone of unpredictable historical contingencies to a neatly delineated "readable space" in which all potential threats or disturbances could be predicted and eliminated.[9] In contrast to the strategic mode of occupying space, which seeks to manipulate and exert a totalizing control over space, a tactical mode of action is "determined by the absence of a proper locus." It has no means to forcefully demarcate space at the expense of other social configurations and must instead "play on a terrain imposed on it and organized by the law of a foreign power."[10] A social configuration adopting a tactical mode of being has no spatial autonomy and lacks the ability to predictably control space in a strategic manner. Any social configuration that operates in this mode will thus embody itself in a transitive and spontaneous fashion, but will never have the enduring characteristics of those who, through manipulation and control, adopt a strategic mode of action.

The state is the social body that which operates in a strategic fashion, since it insists of maintaining its own autonomy, using sheer force to maintain the integrity of its borders against external threats and maximizing the scope of its surveillance over its citizens internally. The state is the epitome of what Augustine calls the *libido dominadi* within the city of Man, since the state "aims at dominion . . . but is itself dominated by that very lust of domination."[11] Capitalism can be seen to extend the strategic logic of the state, particularly because this desire to dominate and keep everything under surveillance is what underpins the logic of capitalism's central tenet, namely commodification. For capitalism to maximise profitability, all things must undergo a process whereby they can be made into an object for exchange. This is a process

---

9. Certeau, *Practice of Everyday Life*, 36–38.
10. Ibid.
11. Augustine, *City of God*, preface.

of rationalization whereby things are turned into commodities by exhaustively determining the dimensions of those things in a way that maintains their integrity as it passes from one set of hands to another. This makes ensuring the manageability and predictability of all objects highly important imperatives, and the transformation of a thing into a clearly delineated, self-contained entity is facilitated by subjecting that thing to a whole array of technologies of organization, management, analysis and supervision. Moreover, these clearly delineated objects have to move within a controlled space, subject to the predictability of regimes of regulation that are crystallized via the clearly defined stipulations of contracts.

In contrast to this, and despite its record to acting to the contrary, the Church can only properly operate when it is outside of this calculus of domination. This is so because, as *Lumen Gentium* states, the Church is only a pilgrim on this earth and thus has no permanent place in the temporal sphere.[12] This eschatological horizon lifts the Church's political horizons beyond those of the particular temporal sovereign in whose territory the Church is in. Instead of the sovereign, the Church must lift its eyes towards the God that exercises sovereignty over all historical space and time. Because of this, the Church treasures but does not fetishize the space it is in, and should not cling to the control of that space. Rather, it should engage in a "relaxed playfulness" within temporal space.[13] As Daniel Bell puts it, the Church should have a way of ordering the life of a polity in a manner that "certainly *occupies* space . . . [but] does not *capture* space in the modern sense of establishing stable borders or barriers."[14] The Church should challenge the strategic manner in which the state tries to control space by declaring of the Body of Christ as its own particular embodied social configuration. However, the Church does not do so in the same manner as the state through the forcible acquisition and management of territory, because the Body of Christ declares the headship of Christ over temporality. Christ is thus the proper *telos* of the Church's social

---

12. *LG*, 7. See also Johnson, *Theology, Political Theory and Pluralism*, 142–43.
13. Mathewes, "Faith, Hope and Agony," 139.
14. Bell, "Jesus, the Jews and the Politics of God's Justice," 102.

Leitourgia, Diakonia, *and* Oikumene

action, in contrast to the state that sees itself and its own survival as its own end. At the same time, the Church's denunciation of the conquest of territory and proclamation of a mode of being distinct from the secular mainstream, cannot amount to a sectarian withdrawal from the secular mainstream in the name of proclaiming a Christian "counter-culture." This is precisely because all of the space the Church operates in is controlled by the state/society/market complex, and also because the Church is a polity without borders in the modern sense. As a configuration adopting a tactical mode of being, the Church cannot retreat because the Church is constantly circumscribed by the complex's strategic domination of social space and therefore has no place to retreat to.[15]

The Church In and Out of Time

Having looked at the different modes by which the Church can more robustly embody itself, the next task is to look at the political consequences of that embodiment for the monopoly of the state/society/market complex. It is important to note that securing space in a way that sets the Church as a political community in its own right can only be complete with a liturgical interruption of an often overlooked dimension of modernity, postmodernity and their subsequent cultural manifestations—time. Thus it is important to first consider how eucharistic space challenges the conception of time within the state/society/market complex. What is important to note, first of all, is that time is not the result of scientific distillation but is "structured through social practices."[16] More importantly, as Scott Bader-Saye notes, the remoulding of time is important in reshaping horizons for the political repositioning of the Church vis-à-vis the capitalist order because "the ways we experience, name and interpret time contribute to the kinds of communities we imagine and inhabit."[17] So what are the

---

15. Hauerwas, *After Christendom?*, 18.
16. Gibbs, "Eternity in History," 127–28.
17. Bader-Saye, "Figuring Time," 98.

Justice, Unity, and the Hidden Christ

contours of time within the practices of the state/society/market complex and that within the body of Christ?

As Stephen Kepnes observes, modern time—sometimes called "clock" time—operates as a seamless stream of repeated units of measure that are constantly being replicated in the present, then irrevocably lost to the past.[18] This is the flattened time that sustains both the state and the market as political communities, since both are founded on confining all reality to the temporal, coupled with the imperative to compress the processes of life into reified commodities whose value can be discerned in a single moment in the present.[19] Eucharistic practice poses a challenge to the status quo because the Eucharist interrupts this flattened time by having eternity "enter history," making the liturgy a simultaneously historical and eschatological event that transforms temporal, and indeed political, experience.[20] The Eucharist's transformation of time is sharpened by Franz Rosenzweig's model of the liturgy as a "reflector which focuses the sunbeams of eternity in the small circles of the year."[21] Through the liturgy of the word, the assembly is told of historical events which are remembered in the pages of scripture. However, these events do not remain in the past, isolated and cut off from the present. Rather, they are brought into the present and lived as if the assembly was living in that "past" moment. In addition, the rituals remind the participant that the point of union is in the supper table of the Lamb of God, an event recorded in the Book of Revelations, to take place in an eschatological future "Kingdom of God."[22] There is thus a simultaneous looking back and eschatological looking forward that makes the modern compartmentalization of past, present and future "lose

---

18. Kepnes, "Rosensweig's Liturgical Reasoning," 115. See also Pickstock, "Liturgy, Art and Politics," 168.

19. Castells, *Rise of the Network Society*. Another incisive look into the changing of the notions of time and its effects on the conception of political society can be found in Anderson, *Imagined Communities*, 22–36.

20. Gibbs, "Eternity in History: Rolling the Scroll," 128.

21. Rosensweig, *Star of Redemption*, 308.

22. Rev 19:9.

Leitourgia, Diakonia, *and* Oikumene

their fixed character."[23] The Eucharist thus interrupts "clock" time because the liturgy presumes a confusion of past, present and future in a single moment.

This is given a sharper focus in the offering of bread and wine. The "in the now" offering of bread and wine casts the participants' minds back to the events leading up to Jesus' death and Resurrection. This can be a simple memorial of a past event, but remember that the endpoint of the eucharistic liturgy is the reception of the Body of Christ. Recall that these elements to the participant are not merely symbolic and pointing to the past, but are real and present "in the now." This reception "in the now" of a real Body of Christ that is the result from that same single sacrifice took place in the past,[24] denotes a bringing forward of that past event into the present. The liturgical sacrifice both as a memorial of Jesus' bounded historical death and resurrection as well as part of a heavenly liturgy collapses the duality between historical (*Kronos*) and eternal (*Kairos*) time.[25] Participants are reminded that the Eucharist is not a replication of a past sacrifice that occurred in a past time, but of one that is continuing outside of time[26] in "the heavenly Jerusalem . . . [with] innumerable angels . . . [and] the assembly of the firstborn enrolled in Heaven."[27] This participation in the *Kairos*, where past, present and future meet, is what brings into the now the seemingly unknown events of the future into a single moment.

The Eucharistic Citizen

The political upshot of this eschatological cutting across of "clock" time is the transformation of the terms of citizenship within any political configuration. Recall that modern notions of

---

23. Kepnes, "Rosensweig's Liturgical Reasoning," 117.
24. Heb 10:11–13.
25. Hahn, *Lamb's Supper*, 117.
26. Heb 9:11–14.
27. Heb 12:22–24.

political community, such as statehood, have no political horizon outside what is circumscribed by "clock" time. On top of that statehood as a form of community building proceeds from the management of populations. Because of these, the only types of people that a state could consider citizens would be those that are alive at a particular moment.[28]

However, because the Eucharist collapses past present and future, the liturgical redefinition of citizenship is given an extra dimension, for citizens of the liturgical *polis* are not only those that partake of the liturgy around the world in the present. The contemporaries of these citizens will include all who share in the body and blood of Christ in the Divine Liturgy. This interrupts modern notions of citizenship because those gathered in the one sacrifice of the Eucharist do not merely include those who participate in it in the present, but also those that have taken part of the liturgy in the past, as well as those that will partake of it in the future.[29]

Eucharist, Idiocy, and Violence

Sacramental practice as exemplified by the Eucharist thereby enacts an ecclesial public space, one that changes the way one looks at the contours of time and the terms of citizenship. If the terms of sociality become transformed in the Eucharist, then the presumptions and cultural logic of acts of social justice cannot help but become similarly transformed. What follows below is the first of three areas wherein a sacramental logic challenges the modern assumptions of the state/society/market complex.

As earlier mentioned, a social compact made out of modern individuals whose autonomy precedes any communal membership can only be effected via a system of contracts. The most fundamental of these contracts is that with the modern nation state, since the mechanisms of the state are in place for the sole purpose of preventing any transgression to the individual's integrity by those that

28. Cavanaugh, *Theopolitical Imagination*, 45.
29. Ibid., 51.

the individual has established contractual relations with.[30] Because of the ontology of violence that creates the individual, its very existence is made dependent on its membership in the state, and the institutionalisation of the relations of violence that entail it. By contrast, eucharistic terms of citizenship interrupt their liberal counterparts firstly by incorporating citizens in a different kind of body: the Body of Christ. It is different because unlike modern notions of political community, the eucharistic Body is one where the heavenly hosts situated outside time break into and blend with those who live in clock time within the same moment.[31] This means that those living in "clock time" are brought into a body wherein also, as John Chrysostom puts it, "our Lord Jesus lies as a slain victim . . . the Spirit is present . . . [and] the Father is [t]here."[32] Because Jesus' identity is bound up to His relations with other persons in the Godhead, the Christian's incorporation into the Body of Christ interrupts liberal citizenship first by declaring that the person in the Body of Christ cannot be the modern autonomous individual. While the modern individual's relations are *extrinsic* to one's identity, being in relation with others is *intrinsic* in the Christian mode of being. The member of the Body of Christ cannot be an isolated monad because one's Christian subjectivity is recognisable only insofar as it is relation to other Christian subjectivities.[33] And precisely because the member of the Body of Christ does not live by itself, in contrast to the contracted individual finding its anchor in the modern state, the member of the Body of Christ can only exist insofar as it is anchored in God. It is pertinent that Sarah Coakley notes that a Christian, particularly a Christian at prayer, is part of a dynamic process of God answering God in and through the one who prays.[34] Christian personhood, like Christian prayer, cannot take place in a condition of idiocy, because there is no space for God in a self-sufficient individual. To let God in,

30. Ibid., 45, 234.
31. Dix, *Shape of the Liturgy*, 252.
32. St. John Chrysostom, cited in ibid.
33. Ward, *Cities of God*, 102–6.
34. Coakley, "Why Three?," 37.

that autonomous individual must be divested of any notion of sufficiency, undergo a self-emptying, and allow God to filter the prayer.[35] Finally, the Eucharist also challenges the primary justification for the creation of the individual, the "state of nature" marked by a fundamental and pervasive relations of violence. This is because the incorporation into the one person of the Godhead is to incorporate one into a social condition of originary harmony.[36]

All these tropes are made explicit when the presbyter, presiding over the Eucharist, asks God that in their participation of the sacrifice of the Eucharist, all participants in the Eucharist be at peace with God and brought together in unity. This liturgical bringing together goes beyond the modern establishment of contractual bridges between individuals, bridges adorned with clearly defined limits to intrusion and suspended by threats of retaliation should those boundaries be breached. Indeed, the Eucharist breaks those barriers down. This occurs via the reception of gifts of bread and wine from the community, offering them as a sacrifice to God and their transformation into into the Body of Christ. From the beginning of these rituals, the barriers between individuals and the gifts they bring are erased, melding the two to the point of confusion. This confusion is demonstrated when the presbyter, in presenting the sacrifice of bread and wine, asks at the same time that the assembly be accepted by God.[37] The fusion of gift and giver is further reiterated when the presbyter later requests that the recipients be transformed into "an everlasting gift to [God]."

In this offering of gifts, the relations of gift are not confined to the individual recipient and God. To paraphrase Augustine, the eucharistic host transforms each recipient into that which is being received, and thus pulls each recipient into the life of the Godhead. Participating in the divine life enjoins simultaneous participation

---

35. Byassee, "Closer Than Kissing," 144.

36. Milbank, *Theology and Social Theory*, 380–438.

37. The complete prayer in the Roman Missal at this point in the Liturgy of the Eucharist goes, "With humble spirit and contrite hear may we be accepted by you, O Lord, and may our sacrifice in your sight this day be pleasing to you, Lord God." See *Roman Missal*, 564.

Leitourgia, Diakonia, *and* Oikumene

with one another. So rather than the modern regard of each other as potential adversaries to be protected from via contractual relations, the liturgical imaginary trains recipients to become gifts to one another. This then raises questions as to the need for the protection of integrity at all costs,[38] even to the point of resorting to violence.

Eucharistic Difference & Liberal Conformity

Eucharistic citizenship also acts as a corrective to the liberal pressure to conform, because the eucharistic apprehension of time transforms the terms of the engagement with difference, creating a foundation for more authentically dialogical relations between different political, cultural or even ecclesial others.

Modern solutions to the engagement with difference, framed within terms of pure immanence, have gravitated around the dichotomy of nihilistic relativism on the one hand and mono-civilisationalism on the other. Because modern solutions to dealing with difference are often set against the backdrop of coexistence of conflicting individuals, difference can only be seen in oppositional terms. In such a context, thinking of and engaging with difference can only come about through a process of "cutting, slicing, arresting, repressing, contracting, splitting [and] subtracting." Like any social engagement, the liberal engagement with difference can only be underscored by violence.[39] The real risk of violence thus gives no right to fully engage the other, but only tolerate it.[40] According to Ghassan Hage, the terms of toleration and the social placements of those to be tolerated are almost always determined by tolerator on its own terms, and imposed on the toleratee involuntarily, further reinforcing inherently dominatory web of relations within liberalism.[41] The paradox is that engaging difference within such a liberal scheme presumes that difference must first be obliter-

---

38. Bader-Saye, "Figuring Time," 96; Cavanaugh, *Theopolitical Imagination*, 118.
39. Cunningham, "Nothing Is, Something Must Be," 94.
40. Minister, "Derrida's Inhospitable Desert," 228.
41. Hage, *White Nation*, 78–104.

ated.[42] This is not to say that the alternatives proposed by what pass for contemporary manifestations of postmodernism resolve the impasse created by modernity. Whilst modernity creates a problematic by demanding conformity, contemporary manifestations of postmodernity by contrast seek to assert the celebration of diversity at all costs. To put it another way, if the modern approach to difference suffers from prioritizing the universal over the particular, the postmodern approach prioritises the particular over the universal. Like their liberal counterpart, postmodern standpoints proceed from the idea of positing difference as inherently antagonistic, and also proceed from the modern original position of a radical atomism. Far from overcoming the shortfalls of modernity, such postmodern variants actually end up replicating the barriers between autonomous individuals. In so doing, such postmodern approaches to difference end up replicating also the relations of nihilistic competition and dominance within liberalism.[43]

The liturgical recovery of participation in divinity and history corrects this logic regarding difference as inherently antagonistic and dominatory because it provides possibilities that transcend a mere "middle ground" compromise between the two poles of nihilism and monolithism. The liturgical ethic would exceed the prescription of mere "tolerance" of different "others" by positing in their stead a logic of incarnation. This logic of incarnation is a critique against the modern subordination of the particular by the universal because, in the Eucharist, the transcendent universal only unfolds itself through the temporal particular. The eucharistic host is more than a mere particular symbol that points to the completely "other" universal, but is truly and particularly that other universal, namely the Body of Christ. The presence of the universal Godhead in the form of that particular bread being broken at that particular eucharistic table affirms the particular as being the key site of the unfolding of the universal.[44] Difference manifest in finitude does not become merely tolerated or obliterated, but

---

42. Bell Jr., "Only Jesus Saves," 216.
43. Cavanaugh, *Theopolitical Imagination*, 120.
44. Ibid., 119.

becomes embraced as a "figural repetition of the other differences" that in turn constitute the universal.[45]

At the same time, the liturgical celebration of finitude simultaneously critiques the contemporary postmodern tendency to prioritise particularly over the universal. The Eucharist, while manifest in that one particular eucharistic table, is not left to reduce to the atomistic relativism. This is because each participant in each liturgical site consumes not separate parts but the whole of a single Body of Christ. All participants are united in that single body of Christ, while at the same time still "inhabiting a particular earthly space."[46] At the same time, the unity of each particular within that single body of Christ would also mean that no one particular eucharistic community can become mutually exclusive of others, in the same way that a postmodern particular only exists as particular when it is in exclusion of others.[47]

The Eucharist also brings to the critique of the post/modern engagement with difference certain nuances to the Church's task of judgement. According to Graham Ward, the logic of incarnation introduces a new dimension to the process of judgement as a necessary ingredient in the Church's engagement with ecclesial others.[48] In the modern mode of relations where horizons are hopelessly marked by pure immanence, each judgement is considered to possess the totality of truth across time and thus renders all judgements on the practices of others as inherently imperialistic or triumphalist. In contrast to this, the Eucharist's declaration of timeless transcendence unfolding in time-bound immanence should aid acknowledgement that each finite encounter with a non-Catholic other has to be infused with "eschatological waiting," as participants of the Eucharist that anticipate the fulfilment of the truth in the liturgy similarly wait for the true meaning of each finite encounter.[49] Also, because the Eucharist includes eucharis-

---

45. Bell, "Only Jesus Saves," 215; Pickstock, "Liturgy, Art and Politics," 172.
46. Cavanaugh, *Theopolitical Imagination*, 119–20.
47. Ibid., 50.
48. Ward, "Christian Act," 43.
49. Ibid., 42.

tic participants in the past, present and future, a non-Christian other can be considered a potential recipient of the Body of Christ and thus a potential citizen of the City of God.[50] When set against this eschatological horizon, the Christian encounter with a non-Christian other could be with be with some who may potentially be a member of the Body of Christ, one of the "people not yet born" and are yet part of God's chosen nation.[51] This is so even when, before Christ comes again, that other remains outside the visible Church.[52] Both these elements enjoin thus a simultaneous rejection of nihilistic relativism, as well as a forestalling any imperial triumphalism.

Eucharistic Economy and Capitalism

If acts of social justice that have their ends circumscribed by capitalism end up being subverted by presumptions of a radical hostility among competitive and self-seeking individuals, then the Eucharist saves the act of social justice by setting that act within a eucharistic economy, one in which social justice can be underpinned by an alternative logic to that in the Market economy.

At one level, a eucharistic economy challenges a capitalist one by cutting across the cornerstone of capitalism's cultural logic, that of commodification or the turning of things into self-sufficient entities with clear barriers between one object and another. Recall that capitalism's logic of commodification extends to the persons engaged in acts of trade, so that each person also becomes a clearly defined, self-sufficient entity. If capitalism operates on the basis of the exchange of alienable objects from individuals in contractual relationships, it would mean a social fabric that maintains very clear boundaries between giver, gift, and recipient. A eucharistic economy distinguishes itself from its capitalist counterpart because the Eucharist does not separate the gift from the transactors.

---

50. Cavanaugh, *Theopolitical Imagination*, 51.
51. Ps 21:31.
52. Cavanaugh, *Theopolitical Imagination*, 48–49.

Leitourgia, Diakonia, *and* Oikumene

Instead, the Eucharist blurs these boundaries such that the reception of the Eucharist makes gifts out of its recipients. The gift is not alienated from the giver, but is joined with the gift. At the same time, the gift is also joined to the recipient. In the *Confessions*, Augustine noted that while Jesus is the food that we feed on, the reception of the Eucharist does not assimilate Jesus and turns him into the recipient. Rather, Jesus in the Eucharist joins with and transforms the receiver into Christ.[53] The consumption of the Eucharist identifies the consumer with that which is consumed.[54] The gift of the Eucharist thereby blurs to confusion the borders that a capitalist economy requires to operate.[55] By collapsing the borders between gift, giver and recipient, the Eucharist cuts across capitalism's borders that maintain the integrity of self-contained commodities and subjects.

Eucharistic practice is also a critique of capitalism at the level of capitalism's narrative of the risk of instability. In modernity, instability is regarded as a social evil to be insured against, and it is the drive to acquire insurance against instability which perpetuates the frantic incursion of capitalist modes of practice within social fabric.[56] In other words, capitalism has reached a phase where it is able to profit from the fluidization and instability it itself has propagated, through what Francois Ewald calls an "insurational imaginary." In such an imaginary, instability is controlled by having all things rationalised into a series of calculable probabilities.[57] In so doing, capitalism is able to simultaneously proliferate factors of risk of instability and sell forms of insurance against that very risk, promising fortresses of stability in a sea of chaos that it itself has created. Set within these horizons, the only alternative to insurance is to become sucked into the chaotic abyss of risk. The Eucharist undercuts this imaginary because, by blurring the distinctions between gift, giver and recipient, the uncertainties

---

53. Augustine, *Confessions*, 124.
54. Marion, *God Without Being*, 156.
55. Cavanaugh, *Theopolitical Imagination*, 48–49.
56. Ewald, "Insurance and Risk," 197–210.
57. Ibid., 198.

of life become posited as inescapable givens built into the social fabric. But rather than resign to chaos, the liturgy couples this collapsing with the Christian narrative of fall, transformation and redemption. This narrative challenges the insurational imaginary by challenging the capitalism's logic of scarcity, which prescribes resistance to the forces that threaten to undermine integrity. This resistance is underpinned by relations of debt, a process that as discussed above, results in modern webs of relations that can only be described as dominatory and violent.

The Eucharist resists capitalism's logic of scarcity and relations of debt with a counter-logic of plenitude[58] that underpins relations of gift and sacrifice. This eucharistic counter-logic is one that could underpin webs of exchanges where people "receive without charge [and] give without charge."[59] The logic of plenitude describes the boundless generosity of God that flows into and transforms all temporal experience, particularly the experience of human suffering which the calculus of scarcity seeks to resist. The Christian calculus of plenitude in one sense welcomes the absorption of harm to security, because historical suffering becomes also the site of historical transformation. It is a narrative that counters the pessimism of the logic of scarcity and thus counters capitalism's exhortation to stockpile against insecurity through relentless accumulation. In so doing the Eucharist interrupts the cycle of capitalism and its logic of competition, domination and eventually violence.

This logic of plenitude is played in the practice of surrendering bread and wine, the products of labor and source of individual sustenance, and diverting instead towards public sacrifice in its liturgical transformation into the Body and Blood of Christ.[60] But this logic of sacrifice and surrender does not leave untouched the issue of temporal sufferings. Because the recipients of the Eucharist are made into the Body of Christ via their consumption of the eucharistic host, the continuation of the Jesus' sacrifice of his body on the altar continues on in the bodies of the Christians that eat

---

58. Bell, "Only Jesus Saves," 211–12.
59. Matt 10:8.
60. Pickstock, "Liturgy, Art and Politics," 166.

of His body.[61] The Latin final liturgical exhortation *Ite Missa Est*— "Go, It is sent"—thereby demands an "unleashing of a multitude of sacrifices" via the participants' lives. Acting as gifts and sacrifices through their exchanges with those around them, the recipients of the Eucharist are called to risk their material and even physical well-being to alleviate the suffering of others.[62]

Conclusion

If practices can form forestructures that influence the *telos* of a given act, then it is possible to consider sacramental practice as similarly constitutive of a set of forestructures and *telos* of the act of social justice. While the previous chapter sought to outline some of the anthropological and political presumptions that are attached to practices circumscribed by a modern context, this chapter showed how these presumptions could be challenged by a eucharistic context.

More specifically it sought to show how acts of social justice could be redeemed in a way that gives full expression to the diversity of manifestations of the Body of Christ within Catholic and non-Catholic ecclesial communions by restoring an ecclesial vision of time and space, marked by a tactical mode of living and an eschatological horizon. Modern presumptions, it was argued, would posit all social action, including social justice and ecumenism within a framework marked by the centrality of the materialistic individual, thereby undermining the ecumenical task by dissolving its communal underpinnings. The Eucharist, however, saves the communal aspect of ecumenism by emphasizing, contra the atomisation of modernity, a Trinitarian logic whereby self is constituted in relation with others. The Eucharist also saves one of the primary concerns about ecumenism, namely the concern for a unity within diversity, by combating modernity's subordination of the particular to the universal, positing in its place a eucharistic

---

61. Augustine, *City of God* 10.6.
62. Pickstock, *After Writing*, 250.

logic whereby the particular is simultaneously the site of the unfolding of the universal. Lastly, it was argued that the Eucharist saves the logic of the act of social justice by positing an alternative form of economics that cuts across the accumulative logic of capitalism. Rather than posit scarcity and fatalism in the face of chaos, the Eucharist posits divine plenitude and the hope for redemption as the primary sociopolitical underpinnings for ecclesial action.

Conclusion

Overview

THE PARABLE OF THE Sower, found in the thirteenth chapter of the Gospel of Matthew, is one of the few parables to be accompanied by an explanation.[1] What the explanation strongly suggests is that when the Word of God is executed, it is never done so in isolation of other concerns, practices and discourses. Rather, the Word of God always finds itself in contact with and moving amongst the material formations in which it is proclaimed. This is most acutely shown in the Parable when the seed fell among thorns. There, the seed of the Word was found to compete with the alternative discourse of the thorns, and a clear manifestation of the Word in the seed's full blooming was not guaranteed. Indeed, in the case of the seed among thorns, the Word became obscured by its alternatives.

Parallels could be found within this episode of the Parable and the analysis of this book, which began with paragraph 12 of *Unitatis Redintegratio*. While the Conciliar celebration of social justice as an avenue for different ecclesial communions to commonly declare Christ seems simple enough, this book has hopefully demonstrated that the simplicity of this paragraph rides upon a complex of cultural and political presumptions that has been rarely explored in the theological literature. In the same way that a ceding of the thorns allowed the choking of the Word, the lack of Conciliar analysis of these presumptions led to the often-too-easy acceptance of a theopolitical complex that dulls the confessionally Christian character of the act of social justice. Because of this,

1. Matt 13:18–23.

the seemingly unbridled confidence of the Council Fathers in the ability to draw on social justice as a wellspring from which greater visible ecclesial communion may seem to be in need of some qualification. This is not to reject the ability of social justice to be an avenue of ecumenism. Rather, this book seeks to draw attention first to the salience of a nexus of theological, anthropological and political presumptions that become institutionalised in a particular form of action, as well as the salience of context in shaping the character of any act. The central task of this book therefore lay in the unpacking, analysing and critiquing of the theopolitical complex that underpinned paragraph 12 of *Unitatis Redintegratio*, and sought to lay out this complex in four stages.

Review

Chapter 1

This book started with an analysis of some of the most salient presumptions assumed by the Council Fathers at the time of the drafting of *Unitatis Redintegratio*. Particular attention was paid to the Conciliar assumption of the neutrality and autonomy of the secular sphere when engaging in Christian action. It considered the genealogy of Catholic philosophical and political thought that enabled the Council Fathers to entertain this notion of secular autonomy, in particularly the split between the temporal and spiritual into two autonomous spheres. Though the temporal was still conceived as being subservient to the spiritual, the latter still had to defer to the former in terms of determining the institutional shape of social actions that took their inspiration from the spiritual sphere.

This book then demonstrated how the legacy of Maritain informed the assumptions adopted by the Council Fathers with respect to culture in the modern world. The evidence to substantiate this conception of culture could be gleaned primarily from key paragraphs of two Conciliar documents that spelled out the contours of the Church's engagement with modernity, namely *Lumen*

Conclusion

Gentium and *Gaudium et Spes*. Though one can be accused of selectively choosing elements of Conciliar documents so as to justify an arbitrarily constructed argument, such accusations can be countered when this selection of Conciliar paragraphs is supplemented by the writings to the same effect by key figures involved in the Conciliar process, in addition to papal thought that was articulated in the leadup to and during the Council's proceedings.

Chapter 2

Having laid out in the elements of the theoretical foregrounding of the Council, the second chapter sought to identify key presumptions entertained by the Council with respect to the Church's engagement with secular culture. It also sought to evaluate their continued relevance in light of our contemporary context. This chapter argued that such presumptions were essentially modern in nature and had a limited ability to operate in a postmodern cultural setting. In addition, this book sought to show how these postmodern lines of argumentation also renders problematic the ability of the Council Fathers to coalesce these modern presumptions with confessionally explicit Christian practice. This book sought to explore both these threads by reference to three theoretical presumptions entertained by the Council.

First, whilst the Council based its findings on the centrality of a unitary Cartesian agent that was stable, autonomous and able to exhaustively know itself and the world around it, this book drew on Foucault's notion of a discursive subjectivity to show that the subject, far from autonomous, could only gain any knowledge by first submitting itself into a series of relation-based social structures, a process which always takes place prior to the subject's knowledge or explicit assent. Because of the constant shifts in context into which the subject is immersed, such a subject was always in the process of formation, never static, and thus never stable. In addition, drawing on Graham Ward, this book also sought to demonstrate that a Christian subjectivity, rooted in a co-abiding in Christ, would find closer correlation to Foucault's discursive subject than the Cartesian knower.

Second, the Council was able to grant autonomy to the secular sphere because it also entertained the notion that the institutional shape of every act contained no ideological content. In the mind of the Council Fathers, the *telos* of the act could only be determined by injecting a cognitive or spiritual addition to the act via the agent. This book demonstrated that the instability of the subject would militate against its ability to infuse a *telos* into the act, and demonstrated that every institutional shape of every institutional act comes already infused with its own ideational content that may make the act itself resistant to any modification by the agent. Indeed, because of the malleability of the discursive subject, the institutional shape of the act may affectively redirect the agent's desires and sociopolitical orientation. In addition, this book also sought to show how the praxiological context of an act, rather than the intentions of the agent, would pay a decisive role in shaping the *telos* of the act of social justice. Under such circumstances, the confessionally Christian *telos* of the act of social justice may become obscured by a non-Christian counterpart, much like the seed being obscured by thorns.

Thirdly, the Council seemed to embrace the notion of the Church being able to act *qua* Church because of the freedom promised by the opening of civil society as an open political forum for participation by all sociopolitical players, free from the coercive force of government. This book analyzed the thought of John Courtney Murray, which was central in guiding the mind of the Council Fathers in embracing civil society as a free space. This book has asserted that, far from being independent of government coercion, the maintenance of civil society actually presumed the logic of the bordered nation state. Indeed, following Michael Walzer, the ability of civil society to fulfil its purpose as a means of building solidarity among diverse agents required the bordered nation state as a more excellent form of sociality than the so called "intermediate bodies" within it. Because civil society presumed a

Conclusion

lack of a common end, the state would always step in as the focal point for the efforts and loyalties of all civil society actors.

In addition to these theoretical concerns, this book also drew attention to a more practical problem that now plagues civil society, namely the capture of civil society to fulfil the ends of capitalism. This book argued that if the Gospel were to be blunted by having to compromise with competing versions of the good within civil society, it would be even more so were it to be subordinated to the *telos* of the market. If the Church were to accept this arrangement, it would do so as a chaplain to the capitalist order, and thereby act to extend rather than challenge it.

Chapter 3

If Chapter 2 cast doubt on the continued applicability of the modern presumptions under-girding paragraph 12 of *Unitatis Redintegratio*, Chapter 3 sought to cast doubt on the compatibility between a Christian anthropology and that presumed by the cultural logic of the market. This book sought to show these inconsistencies at two levels. At one level, it sought to evaluate the ability of social justice to create outcomes consistent with a Christian anthropology, when that act of social justice has been preloaded within the context of the state/society/market complex. At another level, it also sought to evaluate the ecumenical ability of joint social justice projects to build greater communion between ecclesial communities when the *telos* of that act, defined by the state/society/market complex, is not communal, ecclesial or Christian.

Indeed, this book has sought to show that a subordination of the Church to the status of chaplain to the dominant order will actually be harmful to the notion of ecumenism as a means of finding a deep unity within a diversity of ecclesial forms, given that the apparent modern championing of diversity belies its obsession with ensuring a fundamental conformity with a universalised standard, under a thin veneer of external difference. This book has also briefly considered how current manifestations of postmodernism do not overcome this dichotomy of difference and unity, but rather extend the dichotomy between the universal and the particular.

Chapter 4

Another question to address concerns the means by which the Church can carve a mode of action that is properly its own, so as to effect a cultural logic that can properly be called its own. Carving out an ecclesial space is necessary to provide for a confessionally robust *diakonia* as well as found a common wellspring for the Church to draw upon in its attempts to build greater visible communal unity. This book looked at sacramental practice as this very locus of ecclesial action.

This chapter began this analytical thread by looking at the necessity of a tactical mode of the Church's embodiment, contra the state and market's need to control space. This formed the backdrop to an analysis of how the Eucharist melded with a politics of space with eschatological horizons, and in so doing challenged modern notions of citizenship by considering as part of the single *polis* not only of the living (as modern configurations would have it) but also the dead and soon to be born. The Eucharist enacts an ontology of gift that challenges the modern borders necessary for the state/society/market complex to operate. Furthermore, its eschatological horizons reconcile the seeming oppositions between the universal and particular. Finally, this chapter looked at how the Eucharist's embodying of all these elements, and making liturgy part of an ecclesial complex with the act of social justice, redeems the *telos* of the act by repositioning the Church vis-à-vis the state/society/market complex, and deepens the foundations for appreciating the difference within other ecclesial communities even as it asserts its particular and confessionally robust character.

Conclusion

Preview

The critical stance adopted by this book the social justice approach to ecumenism as articulated by paragraph 12 of *Unitatis Redintegratio* might make the reader believe that social justice fundamentally fails the ecumenical cause. That is not the intention of this book, and asserts with Benedict XVI that the Church cannot be conceived as such without *diakonia*. What this book *does* intend to do, however, is expose the complex of unarticulated presuppositions of the approach to *diakonia* that emerged from Vatican II and persist to this day, which are powerful precisely because they are unarticulated and continue to undergird contemporary social practice as a series of self-evident givens. Thus, even when the Church tries to articulate a critique of the institutional arrangements that make up status quo, doing so using these givens as a starting point will eventually result in the critique being coopted by the very thing which the Church is critiquing.[2] These also have an effect on ecumenism, since giving in to these so-called givens means a diluting of the distinctly Christian character of any common witness, in favor of a seemingly more inclusive universalism as is embodied in secular liberal culture.

---

2. This would be so assuming that the Church continues the methodology of analysing cultural issues through the rubric of the "autonomy of culture" as articulated in the earlier chapters of this book, which would eventually mean an ecclesial deference to the discipline of cultural studies in our contemporary context. It is noteworthy that from as early as 1964, Herbert Marcuse launched a scathing critique of the "mass industrial society" that the Council Fathers celebrated in *Gaudium et Spes*. Marcuse argued that this industrialised cultural form had become so all-encompassing it was able to sustain itself by co-opting everything to its logic, including any cultural opposition or critique launched against it. See Marcuse, *One Dimensional Man*.

The fact that the study of culture has now consolidated to become its own discipline has not sharpened its critical edge. Indeed, according to Keith Tester, it has become even more facile, for it assumes fundamentally that "the world is sufficient unto itself and that appearances and fashion are the proper and perhaps only pressing sites of intellectual inquiry." Cultural Studies as a means to critique the status quo thus becomes a fraudulent enterprise, since it "promises critique and delivers accommodation" to the status quo. See Tester, "Culture, Ethics and the End of Sociology," 130.

Justice, Unity, and the Hidden Christ

So long as the Church continues to subordinate its social witness to the dictates of secular culture in the name of granting autonomy to culture, the Body of Christ will eventually declare its role as handmaiden to the capitalist order, via the ceding of space from the latter to the former. As the preceding chapters sought to demonstrate, this makes the Church part of a theopolitical complex that is far from Christian, communal or harmonious. The capitalist order (or any other institutional order for that matter) is no neutral instrument subject to the intentions of the agent. Rather, the capitalist order as part of a modern complex that has absorbed state and society unto itself, acts as a powerful cultural prism that will eventually refract the Church's actions towards the ends of the market so long as it embodies itself only as a subsection of a larger institutional order. In doing so, both the Church's social and ecumenical witnesses become undermined, because the market dissolves the communal bases of organization, institutionalize an anthropology that is anti-Trinitarian, and from that perpetuate relations of vicious domination and competition.

The problem of the application of paragraph 12 of *Unitatis Redintegratio* lies not in the paragraph itself, but rather in the ecclesial acceptance of the theopolitical complex that contextualizes the reading of that paragraph as the only valid hermeneutic. The key to the solution thus lies not in the rejection of the social justice approach to ecumenism, nor in the rejection of paragraph 12. Both these solutions exacerbate the problem by having the Church further cede space to the complete control of secular social configurations, which would further marginalize the Church, as well as deny one of its own key constitutive elements as laid out in *Deus Caritas Est*. A more ecclesial solution hinges on the way in which paragraph 12 is read, in terms of the text itself together with the theopolitical complex, and the practices within which that are attached to the text and give the paragraph meaning. The redemption of the social justice approach to ecumenism lies thus in the rereading of paragraph 12 together with another, more robustly ecclesial, theopolitical complex.

Conclusion

Integral to this rereading is the Church's public re-imagining of itself in relation to other public bodies, an act of what Derrida calls the "recontextualization" of the community, with the community here being the Body of Christ.³ In the context of making the Church's *diakonia* more convincingly embody a common confession of Christ, a Christian recontextualization must be predicated on a more robust embodiment of the Body of Christ vis-à-vis other social bodies. This task requires a radical redefinition of what it means to give autonomy to the secular. This book has implicitly asserted that secular culture as a nexus of embodied or institutionalized practices cannot be seen to be a neutral entity because it actually embodies a secular gospel, and the secular nexus of practices constitutes a secular *leitourgia*.⁴ The spread of the Gospel and the unity of the Church cannot be made dependent on the subjugation of the Church's embodiment in favor of the state/society/market complex.

Instead, the promotion of the Christian *kerygma* that can be recognized as such in a postmodern context requires taking seriously the notion of the Church as a republic, because the Church has its own public reasoning and has its own *res publica*, not only in its works of mercy, but in the works of mercy as tied to the Church's worship. This also requires taking seriously the notion that *diakonia* set within modern institutional forms constitute alternative forms of prayer and worship,⁵ which in turn proclaim a *kerygma*

---

3. Derrida, *Limited Inc*, 146.

4. For a more explicit coverage on the links between practices and the spread of gospels other than the Christian gospel, see Tan, "Reason, Politics and Evangelisation."

5. In his *Commentary on the Sentences of Peter Lombard*, Thomas Aquinas argued that there is a certain continuity between Christian prayer and the works of mercy, so long as the desire for eternal life "persists in all the other works we do in due order." This is why he says that "anyone who never stops acting well never stops praying." See *Commentary on the Sentences of Peter Lombard* Bk. 4, dist. 15, Q. 4/II C, cited in Murray, *Praying with Confidence*, 45–46.

The continuities between prayer and works indicated by Thomas strongly suggest the converse would also be true. The fact that a secular theopolitical complex has redirected the desire of the agent engaged in the act of *diakonia*

other than the Christian one. The ecumenical task thus requires more than merely social justice and more than merely a common doctrinal allegiance. It requires greater scrutiny of the powers and principalities in whose territory the Church must travel as it moves towards the *eschaton*. It requires more discernment as to whether, in reading the signs of the times and in embodying the Gospel in its public practices, the Church is embodying *itself* as an ecclesial public and not subordinating itself to another secular counterpart, letting the latter set the terms of the embodiment of the former. In a way similar to Herbert Marcuse's "great refusal"—the relentless "protest against which that is" and constantly exposing "the mode in which man and things are made to appear to sing and sound and speak"[6]—the Church needs to engage in its own "great refusal" and in so doing be constantly vigilant against the risk of idolatry as it reads the signs of the times.

---

would also mean that Christian prayer would have been substituted by another distorted form of prayer.

6. Marcuse, *One Dimensional Man*, 63.

Bibliography

Althusser, Louis. *For Marx*. London: Cox & Wyman, 1969.
Amato, Joseph. *Mounier and Maritain: A French Catholic Understanding of the Modern World*. Tuscaloosa: University of Alabama Press, 1975.
Ambrozic, Aloysius. "Dialogue with Secularism." In *Culture and Faith*, 8/1:41–46. Vatican City: Pontificium Consilium de Cultura, 2000.
Anderson, Benedict. *Imagined Communities*. London: Verso, 2006.
Arblaster, Anthony. *The Rise and Decline of Western Liberalism*. New York: Blackwell, 1984.
Augustine. *Concerning the City of God Against the Pagans*. Translated by Henry Betteson. Harmondsworth, UK: Penguin, 1976.
———. *Confessions*. Translated by Henry Chadwick. Oxford: Oxford University Press, 1991.
Bader-Saye, Scott. "Figuring Time: Providence and Politics." In *Liturgy, Time and the Politics of Redemption*, edited by Randi Rashkover and C.C. Pecknold, 91–111. Grand Rapids: Eerdmans, 2006.
Ballor, Jordan J. *Ecumenical Babel: Confusing Economic Ideology and the Church's Social Witness*. Grand Rapids: Christian's Library, 2010.
Barth, Karl. *Ad Limina Apostolorum*. Edinburgh: St. Andrew's, 1969.
Baudrillard, Jean. *Symbolic Exchange and Death*. London: Sage, 1993.
Bell, Daniel M., Jr. "Jesus, the Jews and the Politics of God's Justice." *Ex Auditu* 22 (2006) 87–112.
———. *Liberation Theology After the End of History: The Refusal to Cease Suffering*. Radical Orthodoxy. London: Routledge, 2001.
———. "Only Jesus Saves: Towards a Theopolitical Ontology of Judgement." In *Theology and the Political: The New Debate*, edited by Creston Davis, John Milbank, and Slavoj Žižek, 200–230. Sic 5. Durham, NC: Duke University Press, 2005.
———. "The Politics of Fear and the Gospel of Life." *Journal for Cultural and Religious Theory* 8/2 (2007) 55–80.
Benedict XVI. *Deus caritas est: On Christian Love*. 2005. Online: http://www.vatican.va/holy_father/benedict_xvi/encyclicals/documents/hf_ben-xvi_enc_20051225_deus-caritas-est_en.html.

Berger, Peter L., and Thomas Luckmann. *The Social Construction of Reality: A Treatise in the Sociology of Knowledge*. London: Penguin, 1967.

Besançon, Marie. "Relative Resources: Inequality in Ethnic Wars, Revolutions and Genocides." *Journal of Peace Research* 42/4 (2005) 393–415.

Bloch, Ernst. *The Principle of Hope*. Translated by Neville Plaice, Stephen Plaice, and Paul Wright. Cambridge: MIT Press, 1995.

Bourdieu, Pierre. *The Field of Cultural Production: Essays on Art and Literature*. Edited by Randal Johnson. European Perspectives. Cambridge: Polity, 1993.

———. *Outline of a Theory of Practice*. Translated by Richard Nice. Cambridge: Cambridge University Press, 1977.

Boyte, Harry C. and Nancy N. Kari. *Building America: The Democratic Promise of Public Work*. Philadelphia: Temple University Press, 1996.

Bridges, Thomas. *The Culture of Citizenship: Inventing Postmodern Civic Culture*. 2nd ed. Washington, DC: CRVP, 1997.

Budde, Michael. *The (Magic) Kingdom of God: Christianity and the Global Culture Industries*. Boulder, CO: Westview, 1997.

Budde, Michael, and Robert Brimlow. *Christianity Incorporated: How Big Business Is Buying the Church*. Grand Rapids: Brazos, 2002.

Burchell, Graham. "Peculiar Interests: Civil Society and Governing 'The System of Natural Liberty.'" In *The Foucault Effect: Studies in Governmentality*, edited by Graham Burchell, Colin Gordon and Peter Miller, 119–50. Chicago: University Of Chicago Press, 1991.

Castells, Manuel. *The Rise of the Network Society*. Oxford: Blackwell, 1996.

Castoriadis, Cornelius. "Radical Imagination and the Social Instituting Imaginary." In *The Castoriadis Reader*, edited by David Ames Curtis, 319–37. Oxford: Blackwell, 1997.

Cavanaugh, William T. *Being Consumed: Economics and Christian Desire*. Grand Rapids: Eerdmans, 2008.

———. *Theopolitical Imagination: Discovering the Liturgy as a Political Act in an Age of Global Consumerism*. New York: T. & T. Clark, 2004.

———. *Torture and Eucharist*. Challenges in Contemporary Theology. Oxford: Blackwell, 1998.

Certeau, Michel de. *The Practice of Everyday Life*. Translated by Steven Rendall. Berkeley: University of California Press, 1984.

Clapp, Rodney. *A Peculiar People: The Church as Culture in a Post-Christian Society*. Downers Grove: Intervarsity Press, 1996.

Cunningham, Conor. "Nothing Is, Something Must Be: Lacan and Creation from No One." In *Theology and the Political: The New Debate*, edited by Creston Davis, John Milbank, and Slavoj Žižek, 72–101. Sic 5. Durham, NC: Duke University Press, 2005.

Cunningham, David S. "The Trinity." In *The Cambridge Companion to Postmodern Theology*, edited by Kevin J. Vanhoozer, 186–202. Cambridge: Cambridge University Press, 2003.

Bibliography

Davis, Charles. *Theology and Political Society*. Cambridge: Cambridge University Press, 1980.

Derrida, Jacques. *Limited Inc*. Translated by Jeffrey Mehlman and Samuel Weber. Evanston: Northwestern University Press, 1988.

Dix, Dom Gregory. *The Shape of the Liturgy*. London: Dacre, 1945.

Evans, Sara M. and Harry C. Boyte. *Free Spaces: Sources of Democratic Change in America*. New York: Harper & Row, 1986.

Ewald, Francois. "Insurance and Risk." In *The Foucault Effect: Studies in Governmentality*, Edited by Graham Burchell, Colin Gordon and Peter Miller. 197–210. Chicago: University Of Chicago Press, 1991.

Falk, Richard. *Human Rights Horizons: The Pursuit of Justice in a Globalizing World*. London: Routledge, 2000.

Flanagan, Kieran. *The Enchantment of Sociology: A Study of Theology and Culture*. London: Macmillan, 1996.

Flannery, Austin, editor. *Vatican Council II: The Conciliar and Post Conciliar Documents*. Collegeville, MN: Liturgical, 1975.

Foucault, Michel. *Discipline and Punish*. Translated by Alan Sheridan. New York: Vintage, 1979.

———. *The Order of Things: An Archaeology of the Human Sciences*. London: Tavistock, 1970.

Friedman, Milton. *Capitalism and Freedom*. Chicago: University of Chicago Press, 1962.

Gibbs, Robert. "Eternity in History: Rolling the Scroll." In *Liturgy, Time and the Politics of Redemption*, edited by Randi Rashkover and C. C. Pecknold, 127–40. Grand Rapids: Eerdmans, 2006.

Gil, Jose. *Metamorphoses of the Body*. Minneapolis: University of Minnesota Press, 1998.

Gorringe, Tim J. *A Theology of the Built Environment: Justice, Empowerment, Redemption*. London: Cambridge University Press, 2004.

Grenz, Stanley J. *The Social God and the Relational Self: A Trinitarian Theology of the Imago Dei*. Louisville: Westminster John Knox, 2001.

Hage, Ghassan. *White Nation: Fantasies of White Supremacy in a Multicultural Society*. New York: Routledge, 1998.

Hahn, Scott. *The Lamb's Supper: The Mass as Heaven on Earth*. New York: Doubleday, 1999.

Hardt, Michael. "The Withering of Civil Society." *Social Text* 45 (1995) 27–44.

Hauerwas, Stanley. *After Christendom? How the Church Is to Behave if Freedom, Justice, and a Christian Nation Are Bad Ideas*. Nashville: Abingdon, 1991.

———. *A Better Hope: Resources for a Church Confronting Capitalism, Democracy and Postmodernity*. Grand Rapids: Brazos, 2000.

———. *Performing the Faith: Bonhoeffer and the Practice of Nonviolence*. Grand Rapids: Brazos, 2004.

Hekman, Susan J. *Feminism, Identity and Difference*. New York: Routledge, 1999.

Justice, Unity, and the Hidden Christ

Heywood, Andrew. *Political Theory: An Introduction*. 3rd ed. New York: Palgrave Macmillan, 2004.

Horrell, David G. *Solidarity and Difference: A Contemporary Reading of Paul's Ethics*. New York: Continuum, 2005.

Ignatieff, Michael. "Human Rights as Politics." In *Human Rights as Politics and as Idolatry*, 3–52. Princeton: Princeton University Press, 2003.

John XXIII. *Mater et Magistra: Encyclical of Pope John XXIII on Christianity and Social Progress*. 1961. Online: http://www.vatican.va/holy_father/john_xxiii/encyclicals/documents/hf_j-xxiii_enc_15051961_mater_en.html.

———. *Pacem in Terris: Encyclical of Pope John XXIII on Establishing Universal Peace in Truth, Justice, Charity and Liberty*. 1963. Online: http://www.vatican.va/holy_father/john_xxiii/encyclicals/documents/hf_j-xxiii_enc_11041963_pacem_en.html.

Johnson, Kristen Deede. *Theology, Political Theory and Pluralism: Beyond Tolerance and Difference*. Cambridge: Cambridge University Press, 2007.

Johnston, Douglas, and Cynthia Sampson. *Religion, the Missing Dimension of Statecraft*. New York: Oxford University Press, 1995.

Juergensmeyer, Mark. *The New Cold War? Religious Nationalism Confronts the Secular State*. Berkeley: University of California Press, 1993.

Kasper, Walter. *Faith and the Future*. Translated by R. Nowell. London: Burns & Oates, 1985.

Kepnes, Steven. "Rosensweig's Liturgical Reasoning." In *Liturgy, Time, and the Politics of Redemption*, edited by Randi Rashkover and C. C. Pecknold. Grand Rapids: Eerdmans, 2006.

Krieg, Robert Anthony. *Catholic Theologians in Nazi Germany*. New York: Continuum, 2004.

Kymlicka, Will. *Contemporary Political Philosophy: An Introduction*. 2nd ed. Oxford: Oxford University Press, 2002.

———. *Liberalism, Community and Culture*. Oxford: Oxford University Press, 1991.

Lambert, Bernard. "Gaudium Et Spes and the Travail of Today's Ecclesial Conception." In *The Church and Culture Since Vatican II: The Experience of North and Latin America*, edited by Joseph Gremillion, 31–52. Notre Dame: University of Notre Dame Press, 1985.

———. "Gaudium Et Spes Hier Et Aujourd'hui." *Nouvelle Revue Theologique* 107/85 (1985) 321–46.

Langan, John. "Political Hopes, Political Tasks." In *Questions of Special Urgency: The Church in the Modern World Two Decades After Vatican II*, edited by Judith Dwyer, 99–122. Washington: Georgetown Univerisity Press, 1986.

Lubac, Henri de. *A Brief Cathecesis on Nature and Grace*. Translated by Richard Arnandez. San Francisco: Ignatius, 1984.

MacIntyre, Alasdair. *Whose Justice? Which Rationality?* Notre Dame: University of Notre Dame Press, 1988.

Marcuse, Herbert. *One Dimensional Man: Studies in the Ideology of Advanced Industrial Society*. London: Routledge & Paul, 1968.

Bibliography

Marion, Jean-Luc. *God Without Being*. Translated by Thomas A. Carlson. Chicago: University Of Chicago Press, 1991.
Maritain, Jacques. *Integral Humanism*. Translated by Joseph W. Evans. New York: Scribner's, 1968.
———. "Integral Humanism and the Crisis of Modern Times." *The Review of Politics* 1/1 (1939) 1–17.
———. *On the Philosophy of History*. New York: Scribner's, 1957.
———. *Religion and Culture*. Vol. 1, *Essays in Order*. London: Sheed & Ward, 1931.
———. *The Things That Are Not Caesar's*. Translated by J. F. Scanlan. New York: Scribner's Sons, 1931.
Mathewes, Charles T. "Faith, Hope and Agony: Christian Political Participation Beyond Liberalism." *Annual of the Society of Christian Ethics* 21 (2001) 125–50.
———. "Pluralism, Otherness, and the Augustinian Tradition." *Modern Theology* 14/1 (1998) 83–112.
Milbank, John. *Theology and Social Theory: Beyond Secular Reason*. Oxford: Blackwell, 1990.
Minister, Stephen. "Derrida's Inhospitable Desert of the Messianic: Religion Within the Limits of Justice Alone." *Heythrop Journal* 48 (2007) 227–42.
Murray, John Courtney. "Civil Unity and Religious Integrity: The Articles of Peace." In *We Hold These Truths: Catholic Reflections on the American Proposition*, 45–78. Kansas City: Sheed & Ward, 1960.
———. "The Problem of Religious Freedom." In *Religious Liberty: Catholic Struggles with Pluralism*, edited by J. Leon Hooper, 127–98. Louisville: Westminster John Knox, 1993.
Murray, Paul. *Praying with Confidence: Aquinas on the Lord's Prayer*. New York: Continuum, 2010.
Nathan, Laurie. "The Four Horsemen of the Apocalypse: The Structural Causes of Crisis and Violence in Africa." *Peace and Change* 25/2 (2000) 188–205.
Negri, Antonio. *The Politics of Subversion*. Translated by James Newell. Cambridge: Polity, 1989.
Neuhaus, Richard John. *The Naked Public Square: Religion and Democracy in America*. Grand Rapids: Eerdmans, 1984.
Nisbet, Robert A. *The Quest for Community*. London: Oxford University Press, 1953.
Norris, Kathleen. *The Cloister Walk*. New York: Riverhead, 1996.
O'Malley, John. *Tradition and Transition: Historical Perspectives on Vatican II*. Wilmington, DE: Glazier, 1989.
Owen, J. Judd. *Religion and the Demise of Liberal Rationalism: The Foundational Crisis of the Separation of Church and State*. Chicago: University Of Chicago Press, 2001.
Paul VI. *Ecclesiam Suam: Encyclical of Pope Paul VI on the Church*. 1964. Online: http://www.vatican.va/holy_father/paul_vi/encyclicals/documents/hf_p-vi_enc_06081964_ecclesiam_en.html.

Petito, Fabio, and Pavlos Hatzopoulos. *Religion in International Relations: The Return from Exile*. New York: Palgrave Macmillan, 2003.

Pickstock, Catherine. *After Writing: On the Liturgical Consummation of Philosophy*. Challenges in Contemporary Theology. Oxford: Blackwell, 1997.

———. "Liturgy, Art and Politics." *Modern Theology* 16/2 (2000) 159–80.

Pinckaers, Servais. *The Sources of Christian Ethics*. Edinburgh: T. & T. Clark, 1995.

Rawls, John. "The Idea of Public Reason Revisited." In *The Law of Peoples*, edited by John Rawls, 129–80. Cambridge: Harvard University Press, 1999.

———. *Political Liberalism*. New York: Columbia University Press, 1993.

Rosenzweig, Franz. *The Star of Redemption*. Translated by William Hallo. Notre Dame: University of Notre Dame Press, 1985.

Sampson, Cynthia. *Faith Based Diplomacy: Trumping Realpolitik*. Oxford: Oxford University Press, 2003.

Sandel, Michael. *Liberalism and the Limits of Justice*. Cambridge: Cambridge University Press, 1982.

Schall, James V. *Jacques Maritain: The Philosopher in Society*. New York: Rowman & Littlefield, 1998.

Schillebeeckx, Edward. "The Church and Mankind." *Concilium* 1/1 (1965) 34–50.

Schmitt, Carl. *The Concept of the Political*. Translated by George Schwab. Chicago: University Of Chicago Press, 2007.

Scott, James. *Seeing Like a State*. New Haven: Yale University Press, 1998.

Shapiro, Ian. *The Evolution of Rights in Liberal Theory*. Cambridge: Cambridge University Press, 1986.

Sigmund, Paul E. "Maritain on Politics." In *Understanding Maritain: Philosopher and Friend*, edited by Deal Hudson and Matthew Mancini, 153–70. Macon, GA: Mercer University Press, 1987.

Smith, James K. A. *Desiring the Kingdom: Worship, Worldview and Cultural Formation*. Cultural Liturgies 1. Grand Rapids: Baker Academic, 2009.

———. *Introducing Radical Orthodoxy: Mapping a Post-Secular Theology*. Grand Rapids: Baker Academic, 2004.

———. *Who's Afraid of Postmodernism? Taking Derrida, Lyotard and Foucault to Church*. Church and Postmodern Culture. Grand Rapids: Baker Academic, 2006.

Surin, Kenneth. "Marxism(s) and the 'the Withering Away of the State'." *Social Text* 27 (1990) 42–46.

Tan, Matthew John Paul. "Reason, Politics and Evangelisation." *Heythrop Journal* 48 (2010) 1–12.

Taylor, Charles. *Modern Social Imaginaries*. Durham, NC: Duke University Press, 2003.

Taylor, Mark C. *Erring: A Postmodern A/theology*. Chicago: University of Chicago Press, 1984.

Bibliography

Tester, Keith. "Culture, Ethics and the End of Sociology." *New Blackfriars* 78/913 (2007) 129–34.

Thomas, Scott M. *The Global Resurgence of Religion and the Transformation of International Relations: The Struggle for the Soul of the Twenty-First Century*. New York: Palgrave Macmillan, 2005.

Veling, Terry. *Living in the Margins: Intentional Communities and the Art of Interpretation*. New York: Crossroad, 1996.

Walzer, Michael. "The Civil Society Argument." In *Thinking Politcally: Essays in Political Theory*, edited by David Miller, 115–33. New York: Vail-Ballou, 2007.

Ward, Graham. *Christ and Culture*. Challenges in Contemporary Theology. Cambridge: Blackwell, 2005.

———. "A Christian Act: Politics and Liturgical Practise." In *Liturgy, Time and the Politics of Redemption*, edited by Randi Rashkover and C. C. Pecknold, 29–49. Grand Rapids: Eerdmans, 2006.

———. *Cities of God*. Radical Orthodoxy. London: Routledge, 2000.

———. "Postmodern Theology." In *The Modern Theologians: An Introduction to Christian Theology Since 1918*, edited by David Ford, 322–38. 3rd ed. Oxford: Blackwell, 2005.

———. *The Politics of Discipleship*. Church and Postmodern Culture. Grand Rapids: Baker Academic, 2009.

———. *True Religion*. Cornwall, UK: Blackwell, 2003.

Webster, John. "The Human Person." In *The Cambridge Companion to Postmodern Theology*, edited by Kevin J. Vanhoozer, 219–34. Cambridge: Cambridge University Press, 2003.

Weigel, George. *Catholicism and the Renewal of American Democracy*. New York: Paulist, 1989.

Wolin, Sheldon S. *Politics and Vision: Continuity and Innovation in Western Political Thought*. Princeton: Princeton University Press, 2004.

Wright, J. T. *Telling God's Story: Narrative Preaching for Christian Formation*. Downers Grove, IL: Intervarsity, 2007.

Yoder, John Howard. *For the Nations: Essays Evangelical and Public*. Grand Rapids: Eerdmans, 1997.

Žižek, Slavoj. "The 'Thrilling Romance of Orthodoxy.'" In *Theology and the Political: The New Debate*, edited by Creston Davis, John Milbank, and Slavoj Zizek, 52–71. Sic 5. Durham, NC: Duke University Press, 2005.

Zizioulas, John. *Being as Communion: Studies in Personhood and the Church*. Crestwood, NY: St. Vladimir's Seminary Press, 1997.

Index

acts, 32–36, 36–38, 86
　See also Christian acts
acts of social justice, 7, 29, 37–38, 51, 65–66
agency, 29, 32, 34–35
　See also Cartesian agents; Christian agency
aggiornamento (accommodation), 19–21, 24–26
Ambrozic, Aloysius, 19–20
anthropologies
　Christian vs. liberalist/capitalist, 45–61
　difference and conformity, 53–54
　harmony and violence, 49–53
　introduction, 45–46
　liberal idiocy (isolation), 48–49
　summary, 60–61, 87
　Trinitarianism, 47–48
Aristotle, 40
Augustine of Hippo, St., 67, 79
autonomy. *See* culture, autonomy of; secular sphere, autonomy of

Bader-Saye, Scott, 69
Barth, Karl, 19
being, source of, 47–48
Bell, Daniel M., Jr., 52, 68

Benedict, Pope, 64, 88–89
Berger, Peter, 33
body, communicative power of, 34–35
Body of Christ
　appreciation of difference within, 53
　citizenship in, 73–75, 78
　dangers to, 89–90
　as embodying a public space, 66, 68
　eucharistic liturgy and, 71, 80–81
　Pope John XXIII on, 15–16
　unity of, 77
　as a universal, 76
　See also Mystical Body
Bourdieu, Pierre, 33
Brimlow, Robert, 7
Budde, Michael, 7, 43

capitalism
　central tenet of, 67–68
　Church's relationship to, 42–44, 62–64
　Eucharistic economy vs., 78–81
　freedom in, 48–49
　liberalism, relationship to, 46
　liberalist/capitalist anthropology, 48–49, 50–53

101

Index

relations of violence in, 51–52
capitalist order, 90
Cartesian agents (subjects),
    29–32, 36, 85
Cavanaugh, William, 51, 52
charity, ministry of (*diakonia*),
    64–66, 88, 91
Christ
    as *telos* of Church's social action, 68–69
    See also Jesus
Christian acts, 6–7, 62
Christian agency, 29–31
Christian anthropology, 47–49,
    49–50, 87
Christian practitioners, 4
Christian prayer, relationship to
    works, 91n5
Christian subjectivity, 30
Christian unity, 46
Church, the
    capitalist order, relationship
        to, 42–44
    free, presumption of, in civil
        society, 38–42, 86
    positioning of, vs. secular
        culture, 7–8
    as republic, 91
    subordination to liberalism,
        effects of, 60–61
    temporal realm, place in, 17,
        62–64, 68–69
citizenship, 71–72, 73–75
civility, 40
civil society (public square), 3,
    38–42, 86
Clapp, Rodney, 65n5
clock time (modern time), 70–71
Coakley, Sarah, 73
*Commentary on the Sentences
    of Peter Lombard* (Thomas
    Aquinas), 91n5
commodification, 67–68, 78
communicative power of the
    body, 34–35

communion, 47, 48, 59–60
communities of dispositions,
    33–34
community, capitalism's effects
    on, 52
competition, 50, 52
Confessions (Augustine), 79
conformity, 57–60, 75–78
consumer capitalism, 37–38,
    65n8–66n8
consumption, 52
    See also capitalism
contemporary ecumenical
    practice, 2
contractual relationships, 51–52,
    68, 72–73, 73–75
cooperation in social matters,
    1–2
creation, 14–15, 49–50
cultural agendas, 3–4
cultural production, 29
Cultural Studies, 89n2
culture
    approach to, prior to Vatican
        II, 10–17
    assumption of neutrality of, 9
    autonomy of, 24–25, 29, 89n2
    Conciliar definition of, 18
    Mystical Body and, 17–23
cultures, plurality of, 53
Cunningham, David, 56n34

democracy, development of
    state/society/market complex and, 41
Derrida, Jacques, 90
desacralization, 15
desecularization, 2
Deus Caritas Est (Pope Benedict), 64–66
diakonia (ministry of charity),
    64–66, 88, 91
difference, 54–55, 55–57, 75–78
Dignitatis Humanae (declaration
    on religious freedom), 39

Index

dignity, 26
discursive subjects, 29
divine life, participation in, 74–75
divine (supernature), relationship to nature, 10–13
divine/temporal split, 10–13, 14–15, 16–17
Duns Scotus, 36n34

ecclesial publics, building of, 62–82
   community vs. contractual relationships, 72–75
   Eucharistic citizenship, 71–72
   Eucharistic difference and liberal conformity, 75–78
   Eucharistic economy, capitalism and, 78–81
   sacramental locus, importance of, 64–66
   strategic space vs. tactical being, 66–69, 88
   summary, 81–82
   time, nature of, 69–71
Ecclesiam Suam (Paul VI), 16–17, 43
economics, 42–43
   See also market
ecumenism, 3, 7, 53, 89
   See also social justice approach to ecumenism
Enlightenment, Maritain on, 11–12
eternal time (*Kairos*), 71
Eucharist
   eucharistic citizenship, 71–72
   eucharistic economy, 78–81
   gifts and givers in, 74–75, 78–79
   time, transformation of, 70–71, 88
Ewald, Francois, 79

fear, 52
Flanagan, Kieran, 44

Foucault, Michel, 29, 35
free Church in civil society, presumption of, 38–42, 86
freedom, 11, 39
Friedman, Milton, 48

Gaudium et Spes (Pastoral Constitution on the Church)
   on diversity, 53, 54
   on engagement with modern culture, 20–22, 23, 84
   Lambert's influence on, 20
   rationality, support for, 54–55
gifts and givers, in the Eucharist, 74–75, 78–79
Great Refusal (Marcuse), 92
guarding, 35

Hage, Ghassan, 75
Hardt, Michael, 41
harmony, of Christian anthropology, 49–50
Hauerwas, Stanley, 65
heavenly benefits, 23
hierarchies, 56
Hobbes, Thomas, 50
Holy Spirit, 55
human rights discourse, 48–49

idiocy (isolation) of liberal anthropology, 48–49
imaginaries, 6, 30, 35, 37, 79–80
imaging (of humans to God), 47
incarnation, logic of, 76
individualism, 50–51, 51–52, 57–60
individuals, 35–36, 48
individual will, realities and, 36–37
institutional acts, presumption of neutrality of, 32–36, 43, 86
institutional orders, nature of, 90
insurational imaginaries, 79–80
Integral Humanism (Maritain), 10–11
isolation (idiocy), 48, 73–75

Index

Jesus
  on self-sufficiency, 31
  See also Christ
John Chrysostom, St., 73
Johnson, Kristen, 57
John XXIII, Pope, 15–16

Kairos (eternal time), 71
Kasper, Walter, 19
Kepnes, Stephen, 70
kerygma-martyria (proclaiming the word of God), 64, 65, 91–92
knowledge, 30–31, 33
Krieg, Robert, 10
Kymlicka, Will, 57

Lambert, Bernard, 20
leitourgia (sacramental practice), 64–66, 88, 91
liberal conformity, 57–60, 75–78
liberal individualism, 57–60
liberalism, 46, 53–54, 54–55
liberalist/capitalist anthropology, 48–49, 50–53
libido dominadi (lust of domination), 67
Locke, John, 50
logic of scarcity, 50, 52, 80
Luckmann, Thomas, 33
Lumen Gentium (Second Vatican Council), 20, 21, 68, 84

mankind, agency of unity of, 14
Marcuse, Herbert, 89n2, 92
Maritain, Jacques, 10, 12–15, 22
market
  anti-Christian nature of, 46, 90
  Church, influence on, 38–39, 87
  collapse of state and society into, 41–42
  competition in, 52
  See also capitalism
Mater et Magistra (John XXIII), 15–16
Mathewes, Charles, 61
mercy, works of, relationship to prayer, 91n5
migration, agency and, 29–30
ministry of charity (diakonia), 64–66, 88, 91
modern culture, locus of Church's engagement with, 23
modernity, 10–11
modern states, 13
modern time (clock time), 70–71
Murray, John Courtney, 39, 86
Mystical Body
  Conciliar approach to culture and, 17–23
  divine/temporal split and, 10–13
  immediately prior to Vatican II, 13–17
  New Christendom, continuity with, 16
  See also Body of Christ

nation states, 37–38
Negri, Antonio, 41
Neuhaus, Richard John, 40–41
neutrality, of institutional forms of acts, 32–36
New Christendom, 12, 16
non-Christian others, 78
Norris, Kathleen, 57

O'Malley, John, 18

Pacem in Terris (John XXIII), 16
Panopticon, Foucault's account of, 35
Parable of the Sower, 83
paragraph 12 of Unitatis Redintegratio
  context for, 3, 24–25

Index

on cooperation in social matters, 1–2
nature of problem of, 90
presumptions of, 83–84
on social justice approach to ecumenism, 2, 27–28
subjectivism of, 23
particular vs. the universal, the, 76–77, 87
Paul VI, Pope, 16–17, 42–43
performances, 36
plausibility structures, 33
plenitude, logic of, 80
plurality of cultures, 53
political liberalism, 4
politics of belief, 6
power, relations and, 56
Practice of Everyday Life, The (Certeau), 66–67
practices, 33–34
prayer, relationship to works, 91n5
presuppositions to Vatican II, 27–44
   acts, isolated *telos* of, 36–38
   acts, neutrality of institutional forms of, 32–36
   Cartesian agent, presumption of, 29–32
   Church as chaplain to capitalist order, 42–44, 87
   free Church in civil society, presumption of, 38–42
   introduction, 27–28
   power of, 89
   summary, 45–46
Primacy of the Supernatural (*Things that are Not Caesar's*, Maritain), 12
public square (civil society), 3, 38–42, 86

rationality in liberal theory, 54–55
Rawls, John, 58–59
realities, cause of, 36–37

reasonableness, 58–59
recontextualisation, 90–91
reform Catholicism, 10
relations
   in Christian anthropology, 49–50
   of debt, 80
   of difference, 56–57
   importance, 47–48
   in liberal anthropology, 50–51, 53
   power and, 56
republics, Church as, 91
risks, in liberal anthropology, 50
Rosenzweig, Franz, 70
Rowland, Tracey, 18–19, 20

sacramental practice (*leitourgia*), 64–66, 88, 91
Sandel, Michael, 60
scarcity, 50, 52, 80
Schillebeeckx, Edward, 14–15
Schmitt, Carl, 50n14
sciences, 55
Scoot, James, 40
Second Vatican Council (Vatican II). *See* anthropologies, Christian vs. liberalist/capitalist; ecclesial publics, building of; *Gaudium et Spes*; presuppositions to Vatican II; *Unitatis Redintegratio*
secular sphere, 6–7, 19
secular sphere, autonomy of
   Conciliar understanding of, 23, 24, 25, 42, 43, 84
   credibility of idea of, 29, 91
   Lambert on, 20
   Lumen Gentium on, 21
   Maritain's belief in, 9, 11, 12, 15, 16
self, 30, 32, 47
self-sufficiency, of Cartesian subject, 30
Sigmund, Paul, 10

Index

Smith, James K. A., 65n8–66n8
social ills, 23
social imaginaries, 6, 30, 35, 37
social justice, 4, 25
social justice approach to ecumenism, 2, 24–28, 90
social justice projects, 3–4
social matters, cooperation in, 1–2
social spaces (social universes), 3–4, 34
society, 35–36, 41–42
  See also public square
Sower, Parable of the, 83
spaces, 3–4, 34, 66–69, 88
  See also public square
spiritual realm. See *entries beginning "divine"*
spiritual/temporal divide, 10–13, 14–15, 16–17
state, the
  citizens of, 72
  civil society, relationship to, 40–41, 86
  collapse into market, 41–42
  free civil society and, 39
  as protector of individuals, 51
  role in natural realm, 12–13
  strategic mode of operation, 67–68
  See also state/society/market complex
state of nature, 50
state/society/market complex, 41–42, 69–70, 87
subjectivity, 30–31
subjects, 29–30, 85
  See also Cartesian agents (subjects)
supernature. See divine
Surin, Kenneth, 41

Taylor, Charles, 6, 30
telos of acts, context of, 32, 36–38, 86

temporal realm (nature), 6–7, 10–13, 19, 62–64, 68
temporal/spiritual divide (divine/temporal split), 10–13, 14–15, 16–17
Tester, Keith, 89n2
theories, relationship to practices, 33
Thomas Aquinas, 91n5
time, 69–71, 77, 88
Trinitarianism, 47–49, 55–57
Trinity, nature of, 47, 55–56

Unitatis Redintegratio, 9–26
  aggiornamento and, 24–26
  on cooperation in social matters, 1
  culture, approach to, prior to Vatican II, 10–17
  on faith and markets, 42
  introduction to, 9
  Mystical Body and approach to culture, 17–23
  Mystical Body and divine/temporal split, 10–13
  Mystical Body immediately prior to Vatican II, 13–17
  paragraph 12, 1–3
  See also paragraph 12 of *Unitatis Redintegratio*
the universal, the particular vs., 76–77, 87

Vatican II (Second Vatican Council). *See* anthropologies, Christian vs. liberalist/capitalist; ecclesial publics, building of; *Gaudium et Spes*; presuppositions to Vatican II; *Unitatis Redintegratio*
violence, 50–53, 75

Walzer, Michael, 40, 86
Ward, Graham

106

on acts, meaning of, 37
on Christian agency, 29–30
culture, Trinitarian reading of, 56
on discursive subjects, 29
on knowledge, 30–31
on logic of incarnation, 77
politics of belief, use of phrase, 6
on relations of difference, 56

Weigel, George, 40–41
will, 36–37, 48
William of Ockham, 36n34
Word of God, execution of, 83
works, relationship to prayer, 91n5

Yoder, John Howard, 43–44

www.ingramcontent.com/pod-product-compliance
Lightning Source LLC
Chambersburg PA
CBHW050841160426
43192CB00011B/2111